# WHERE ARE WE GOING TODAY, LORD?

JIM OSTEEN

ISBN 979-8-89345-016-3 (paperback)
ISBN 979-8-89345-017-0 (digital)

Copyright © 2025 by Jim Osteen

All rights reserved. No part of this publication may be reproduced, distributed, or transmitted in any form or by any means, including photocopying, recording, or other electronic or mechanical methods without the prior written permission of the publisher. For permission requests, solicit the publisher via the address below.

Christian Faith Publishing
832 Park Avenue
Meadville, PA 16335
www.christianfaithpublishing.com

Printed in the United States of America

To our Lord and Savior and to His glory.
In grateful appreciation to my beautiful wife, Lou Ellen, for more than fifty years of faithfully serving by my side. She is truly a servant of God and the helpmate I needed for this journey together.

# Foreword

"HEY THERE, FELLA"—THOSE were the first words I recall Jim Osteen said to me on that bright Sunday morning nearly forty years ago. He was walking up the sidewalk at a little country church that I was a member of on the day of his trial sermon. The man I met that day became my pastor, my friend, my confidant, and my mentor.

Preacher Jim, as we all called him, had an easy way about him. His stories and illustrations had us hanging on every word on Sundays. He would catch our attention with a good story and then drive home a point, leaving some powerful truth anchored our spirit.

Nothing captures the attention and the imagination like a good story, especially when the story is a down-home tale that brings a smile to your face. My grandfather would regale us for hours with his homespun humor. Andy Griffith and Barney Fife entertained us for years with that same kind of storytelling.

And nothing drives home a spiritual point in a sermon like an illustration. People perk up, ears open, and hearts soften when the pastor tosses in a good illustration. Jesus Himself used this same method to capture His audiences and lead them to a lofty spiritual reality. We call His stories parables.

Whether you're a pastor, Sunday school teacher, or Bible teacher looking for a little inspiration or somebody looking for a good story and a laugh—something positive to cling to in the torment of negativity that we experience every day—you've come to the right place. You will be inspired. You will be educated. You will be blessed!

## JIM OSTEEN

Find you a recliner or a front porch swing and sit a spell. Slow down, relax, and be refreshed by these simple yet powerful pages.

Rev. Alex D. Henderson, Senior Pastor<br>
Chestnut Ridge Baptist Church<br>
Laurens, South Carolina

# 1

# Interruption or Opportunity

## John 15:1–15

DO PEOPLE ANNOY you? Do they?

Imagine Jesus wanting to be alone with His disciples. He needed time to teach them.

We are told He was alone with His disciples when here came five thousand men plus women and children. That's what I call an interruption.

I remember our first parsonage. It was a nice brick home with a large basement for the kids to play in. We had two toddlers at the time. While we enjoyed the house, I can't help but feel that when the house was built, they were installing the plumbing and telephone at the same time. They had to have been. I believe they got the wires and pipes crossed because every time I got into the shower, what happened? The phone rang (this was long before cell phones).

I sing in the shower, actually sound good in the shower. I would be all soaped up, really enjoying myself when—*What's that?* Ring number one. As I turned the water off, I would hear ring number two. I would pull the curtain back and step out of the tub as ring number three went off. I'd turn left and step into the hallway. Ring number four. Now the race was on. I would run down the hall and make the left turn into the bedroom. Ring number five. Almost there. I would reach and pick up the phone as I heard ring number six. As I said,

"Hello," trying not to sound out of breath, I would hear the sound many of you have heard. *Click*. They hung up. I didn't quite make it in time. So there I was, dripping water and suds on the carpet.

I would turn and head back to the shower, adding to the water trail I had already left on the carpet. I would get back into the shower but not singing this time. I'd lost the mood. Then my dear sweet wife would come in and ask, "Who got all this water on the floor?" as if someone else had been taking a shower and running up and down our hallway. She knew it was me.

Now I was in trouble, and it wasn't my fault. She wanted me to be clean. The folks at church wanted me to be clean. I wanted to be clean. That's what I was trying to do when I was interrupted. Do people annoy you?

At our second parsonage, I was at home one Saturday, all by myself. My wife and kids had gone out, and I was home alone. This particular Saturday was a college football lover's dream. I was watching two games at once. When the team was in the huddle on one station, they were running the play on the other station. I was praying, "Lord, please don't let there be a penalty or something to get these games out of sequence." This was great.

Then I heard the sound. Oh, no, not now. It was a knock at the door. Maybe it was just someone selling fruit or something for the school. When I opened the door, there was a lady about fifty years old. I could tell she had fixed herself up to go somewhere, but her do was now a *don't*. She looked distressed, not looking good for my ball games. She spoke before I had a chance to speak to her.

She said, "Are you the pastor of the church up the street?" So much for the ball games. I said, "Yes, I am. What can I do for you?" As I spoke, I noticed a car in front of the house. If that was her car, and she needed someone to fix it, I was not the one. I could drive anything and take care of them, but I am not a mechanic. She told me she had a flat tire and had tried to change it but couldn't get the "thingy," as she said, to turn. Then she said, "Could you help me?"

I said, "Sure thing. Let me get my shoes" (I was barefoot in the house).

As I stepped back inside to get my shoes, she asked, "You weren't doing anything, where you?"

I said, "No, I was just sitting here wishing I had someone I could help."

I have changed a lot of tires. I was good at it. It only took me a few minutes to change a tire. But that day was a little different. You see, as I was walking to the car, it dawned on me (probably the Holy Spirit) that this lady was not going anywhere until I changed her tire. I wasn't as strong and quick as usual in turning that "thingy," as she called it. After a little chatter, while I was changing the tire, I asked her, "Do you come down this road often?"

She said no and explained where she was headed. I asked her if she had ever heard about the Roman road.

She said she had never been to Rome or driven on any road called the Roman road that she knew of. Then as I was changing the tire, I took through the Roman road. The Roman road is a way of sharing the gospel message using several verses of Scripture from the book of Romans. I have used it often. While she did not accept Jesus that day, it was clear the Holy Spirit was working on her. I gave her some information and encouraged her to attend a Bible-believing church when she returned home.

The ball games I was watching were not so important anymore. We often pray for opportunities to share the gospel or to minister to someone. The Lord hears our prayers and sends someone our way or sets up an opportunity, and we see it as an interruption.

We are often tempted to see these as interruptions rather than opportunities to minister in His name.

People are crying out, and we aren't listening because we are too caught up in ourselves and what we are doing.

# 2

## The Great Pretenders

### Matthew 7:13-23

MANY, MANY YEARS ago (1970s), I was serving as a minister of music and youth. I really loved the pastor I was serving under and learned a lot from him. He had a major impact on our ministry. So you can understand it hurt when a rumor began to spread about him.

I know it's hard for you to imagine a rumor floating around a church, but it does happen. The church seemed to be evenly split as to whether or not it was true. Even my wife said she thought it was true. I didn't think so.

Well, finally one of our youth decided he would settle the matter. The youth were having a skating party at the local skating rink. The pastor always supported the youth and would usually make an appearance at the youth events even if he didn't stay.

What was the rumor? The rumor was that the hair on his head was not his. My wife said it had to be a toupee because his hair was always perfect. It was never out of place.

The pastor took his place along the wall surrounding the rink (I call it the crash wall because people often crash into it to stop). He had his elbows resting on the top of the wall. One of the youths, as he was skating by, raised his hand to give the pastor a high five as he skated by. The pastor leaned out over the wall and held up his hand to tap the youth's hand as he went by. Just before hitting hands, the young man reached forward and grabbed a handful of the pastor's hair. One of two things was about to happen. If the pastor's hair is real and growing from his head, the young man would suddenly have his legs skate out from under him as he was jerked back from grabbing the pastor's hair. He won't be able to turn loose before his legs would go out from under him. He was going to look very foolish lying on the floor. But if the pastor was wearing a toupee, the young man would never slow down as he continued around the rink with a handful of hair.

The young man never slowed down as he pulled the pastor's hair from his head. He continued around the rink and presented the toupee back to the pastor. The pastor showed a lot of grace that day as he simply returned the hair to the top of his head.

But people are not the only ones who wear artificial hair. My uncle had several horses, including his ribbon-winning Tennessee walking horse. Her name was Delightful Surprise. She was a beauty and a smooth ride. As a young boy, I would often help with the horses. But have you ever noticed how the tail of a show horse stands up so pretty? That's because they are not all real. In my uncle's tack room was a row of saddles, a row of bridles, a display of the ribbons his horses had won, and a row of artificial tails. Before going to the show, we would groom the horse and pick out a tail that matched the color of the horse. We would attach it to the real tail and brush it in. Guess who often got the job of working on that end? Me. While my uncle would be brushing the rest of the horse, I would be getting the tail just right. My uncle would always tell me the same thing, "Be careful, and don't let her kick you in the mouth." She never did. She was very gentle and well-trained. But if she had, and I lost a tooth, I would simply go to the dentist and get an artificial tooth.

And, ladies, why do you get all upset when you break a nail? "Oh, I broke my nail." No problem. Just go to Walmart and get some super glue and some of those artificial nails and stick them on. Problem solved.

Now they are messing with food. We have artificial sugar. You can get a variety of colored packs (pink, yellow, blue). The interesting thing is that after telling us not to use real sugar, they are now saying the real thing is better for us than the artificial. There is even artificial salt and artificial butter.

I love a fried bologna sandwich. But now, it might not be the real thing. It may look like bologna, smell like bologna, even taste like bologna, but it's not. It's turkey bologna.

There is nothing like bacon to go with your eggs and grits for breakfast. But is it bacon? It may look like bacon, smell like bacon, and even taste like bacon. But it's actually turkey bacon. It's the same thing with ham—turkey ham. I love turkey. It's hard to beat turkey and my wife's dressing. But when I want bologna, I want bologna. And when I want bacon, I want bacon.

Many will be putting up artificial Christmas trees before long. They don't smell as good as the real thing.

Everywhere we turn, there are artificial things. Some of them are good. But not only are our stores filled with artificial things, but also the church is filled with artificial Christians, what I call the great pretenders.

Matthew 7:13–23 gives a stern warning to these great pretenders: "I never knew you."

It's not just a religious ceremony, whether traditional, contemporary, or blended. It is a matter of the heart.

While I was serving in the Marine Corps Reserve, I got on a plane to fly with several other Marines to San Diego for special training. After landing in San Diego, we got on a landing craft and went to San Clemente Island, about sixty miles off the coast.

As we were waiting to board the plan for San Diego, one Marine told me he was a deacon in his church. I was happy to know I would have another Christian with me. Another Marine joined us just before takeoff. I sat between them.

As we were taking off, the marine who had just joined us bent over me and asked the deacon if he was going to cheat on his wife if we got any free time when we returned from the island to San Diego. I thought, *You just asked the wrong person. He is a deacon in his church, and he is going to let you know he wouldn't do such a thing. And I'm going to support him when he does.* I leaned back and waited for the deacon's answer.

He asked, "How far is San Diego from here?"

"I think it's about three thousand miles."

The deacon said without any hesitation, "That's legal separation. Of course, I'm going to cheat on my wife." And he did. After a difficult time on the island, we got a few days off, and he cheated.

It was on a Monday that we were taking off. On Sunday, he was probably in church, praying the prayers, talking the talk, dressing the dress, maybe sitting on committee meetings, discussing the activities and business of the church. He may have been taking up the offering or teaching a class. But the rest of the days, he was not walking the walk. He was not walking with Jesus.

He was one of the great pretenders of whom there are way too many.

I once heard Dr. Don Wilton of First Baptist Church, Spartanburg, say the reason we have so many churches in conflict is because we have unspiritual people making spiritual decisions.

> He who says, I know Him, and does not keep His commandments, is a liar, and the truth is not in him. But whoever keeps His Word, truly the love of God is perfected in him. By this we shall know that we are in Him. He who says he abides in Him ought himself also to walk just as He walked. (1 John 2:4–6)

I can assure you that the deacon was not walking as Jesus walked. He had the title of deacon but not the true heart of a deacon.

# 3

## Corn Bread and Icing

### Matthew 7:13–23

THERE WAS A bake sale being held at the church to raise money for missions. People brought brownies, cakes, cookies, etc. They were auctioning off the cakes. Two of the ladies got into a bidding war for one of the cakes. The bids were getting way up there, way more than anyone would ever pay for a cake. It began to appear that they were not just bidding for the cake to help missions but also to beat the other one.

The cake they were fighting for (excuse me, bidding for) had chocolate icing. It really looked good, and the lady who made it was known for her good cakes. One lady asked if it was a yellow or white cake. They were told it was a yellow cake covered with chocolate icing. Finally, the bidding ended, and the highest bidder picked up her cake.

There was plenty of coffee, tea, soft drinks, etc., so most people opened up what they had bought, and everyone (well, most everyone) shared the sweets with a good time of fellowship. The lady who had lost the bidding for the cake asked the lady who got it if she could have a piece. The lady with the cake said, "No way. You caused me to pay too much for this cake." She took her cake, got into her car, and started her drive home. As she was driving, she was probably thinking about how good that chocolate cake was going to be.

When she got home, she put a pot of coffee on and went to change clothes while the coffee was brewing. As she returned to the kitchen, she could smell the aroma of the freshly brewed coffee. She poured herself a cup and unwrapped the cake. Her mouth was probably watering as she could almost taste it. She took her cake knife and started to cut the cake. She immediately knew something was wrong. It seemed a little hard, too hard for a freshly made cake. She went ahead and cut out a piece of cake. As she pulled it away from the rest of the cake, her heart sank. It was corn bread. It was two round cakes of corn bread stacked on top of each other and covered with icing. If you want to decorate a pretty cake, use corn bread. It's firm and will hold up to spreading the icing.

It was yellow on the inside, just like the lady who made it said it was. It looked like a chocolate cake. It smelled like a chocolate cake. But it was not what it appeared to be; it was corn bread and icing.

There are many, too many, in our churches whose inward nature has not changed. They have no personal relationship with Jesus. They are just corn bread and icing.

Has there been an inward change?

> You shall know them by their fruit. (Matthew 7:16)

> You shall know them by their fruit. (Matthew 7:20)

One morning, as I was in my office, our youth minister came in. He was all excited. I could tell he was anxious to tell me something. I thought it would have something to do with our youth program as things were going well. This was this young man's first ministerial position. He was eager to learn. I was happy to have him as an associate. I was not expecting what came next.

I laid my pen down to give him my full attention. He said, "Preacher, I'm saved!"

I said, "I know you are."

He said, "No, you don't understand. I got saved this weekend."

I said, "Sit down, and let's talk." I was anxious to hear his story. He told me that when he was a little fellow, he was standing next to his mother in church while they were singing the invitation song. His mother leaned down to him and said, "Don't you want to go down and speak to the pastor?" He wanted to please his mom and liked the pastor, so he nervously headed down the aisle. He said he didn't know what he was going to say when he got there. As he got close, the pastor reached out and took him by the hand and spoke. This took the pressure off him trying to think of something to say. The pastor asked, "Are you wanting to get baptized?"

He said, "Sure." He thought that would be fun. He had seen others go into the pool and thought he would too. He said, when the invitation ended, the pastor stood him up before the congregation and told them he'd been saved. All the people came by, telling him how happy they were he'd been saved. He assumed he was.

He said he had realized this weekend, even though he was in church every week and serving as a leader, he'd never actually given his life to Christ. But now he was saved.

We have too many in churches like him, who have never really given their lives to Christ. They are just corn bread and icing. Maybe this is why we have so many inactive members.

When I meet people, and they find out I'm a minister, they often ask, "How many members do we have?" They tend to judge according to the size of the church. Through the years, I have been blessed to pastor large churches with full staff, as well as small churches without staff. I can assure you that in God's eyes, all churches and ministers are important, no matter what size.

When they ask how many members we have, I always answer with a question I once heard another pastor use, "Do you want my bragging numbers or my actual numbers?" My bragging numbers are the ones listed on the church roll, which usually about doubles the number you see on Sunday. Many of the rest are corn bread and icing. There are those who are homebound, sick, unable to come. But most of those who are not coming have no trouble going anywhere else they want to go. God knows the difference.

# WHERE ARE WE GOING TODAY, LORD?

There is a big difference between knowing about someone and really knowing them. There is a big difference between knowing about Christ and really knowing Him.

We had finished leading revival meetings in Arkansas and were headed to Oklahoma. From there we would go to Seattle, Washington, and then back to North Carolina. From North Carolina, we would return to South Carolina, just in time to spend Thanksgiving with our family.

Saturday, as we were traveling on the interstate, our engine blew. It was dead.

I coasted over to the side of the road. When the tow truck arrived (our motor home required a tow truck for tractor-trailer rigs), I told the driver I needed it towed to someone who could change a motor home engine. He told me he knew just the person. It was a car dealership that had experience in changing all kinds of engines.

It was dark when he pulled us into the dealership. Everyone was just about gone. I was getting concerned about making it to the church in Oklahoma in time. The manager assured me they could handle the job. The tow truck driver offered to pull us all the way to the church in Oklahoma for just under one thousand dollars. I said we would pass on the offer. That turned out to be a big mistake. I should have taken him up on the offer.

The dealership didn't have any cars to loan or rent. They called the fellow at another dealership, who could rent us a car. By now it was getting pretty late, so we had to wait for him to come and open his dealership back up. The tow truck driver dropped us off at the truck stop while we were waiting for the man to come and pick us up with the rental car. We were able to get something to eat and take a shower at the truck stop.

It was a little past midnight when we finally got back on the road. I called the church and explained the situation. I told him I thought we would make it in time for the Sunday morning service but would not be able to stay in our motor home as planned. He said someone in the church had a vacant house, fully furnished, that we could use that week. Great! The Lord had already taken care of our need. Now if we could just make it to the church in time for the services.

We drove the rest of the night. We arrived at the house a little before nine o'clock, Sunday morning (and we found it without GPS systems like we have now). We would not be there for Sunday school, but we would be there in time for the worship service. Lou Ellen was to sing and lead the children's time, and I was to preach. When we walked into the church, we both were tired from being up all night and from all that had happened, but we were ready to go.

The services went well. We slept that afternoon and were back at the church that night for the evening service. I was feeling good about everything. I would call and check on the motor home in the morning.

Monday morning, I called and was assured that they had assigned our motor home to a mechanic and that he would have it ready in a few days. Timing was going to be close. Originally, we were planning on leaving Oklahoma on Thursday morning after finishing the revival on Wednesday night. That would give us Thursday, Friday, and Saturday to make the drive to Seattle. The revival would still end on Wednesday night, but would we have our rolling house to make the trip?

It became evident on Tuesday that we were not going to have the work finished. When I called and asked to speak to the mechanic working on the motor home, they told me he was out that morning but was going to work that afternoon and late that evening. The receptionist just didn't seem that convincing to me.

Wednesday morning, they told me it was not going to be ready before the weekend. So much for driving to Seattle and staying in our motor home. I had actually been looking forward to that drive. We would have to fly. This is not the way we had planned, and expenses were piling up.

Someone in the church we were at told us the plane tickets were taken care of. They wanted to purchase them for us as a way of supporting God's work. There were not any flights from where we were in Oklahoma. We also had a rental car we needed to return. Thursday morning, we got up early and drove back to Arkansas to return the rental car. We were taken to the airport.

## WHERE ARE WE GOING TODAY, LORD?

I had called the pastor in Seattle and told him about our situation and that we would need a place to stay. He gave us a choice. He said the church would put us in a hotel for the week, or we could stay in a church member's house, who was out of town for a few weeks. He had called them and explained the situation, and they said it would be fine. They would be back and would join us for our last two nights at the house. The house had a large deck off the back with a beautiful view of Mt. Rainier. We chose the house, which would save the church the expense of the hotel, plus we would enjoy the view each morning. I would enjoy my coffee on the deck. The revival would be Sunday to Wednesday, and then we would stay and lead the services again the next Sunday. On Saturday, following the revival, a couple took us around to see the sights. Not only did the Lord bless our time of revival there but gave us a great time of meeting new friends and enjoying His creation.

However, despite the great week we were having, things were not going so well for the motor home. I would call but was never able to talk with the mechanic. Finally, I reached him toward the end of our stay in Seattle. He apologized for being so hard to reach but was going to school in the mornings. I thought it was great that he was going to school until he told me what he was taking. He was taking automechanics. He said his professor told him it was pretty neat that the *first* engine he ever changed was going to be a motor home. I tried to hold back my panic as we talked. Our first motor home had a gas engine that was in the front. He said it took him a couple of days to figure out how to get it out. He said he finally got it out and another one put in. It should be ready when we get back. I didn't feel good about the motor home but knew God had taken care of everything else, and He was certainly able to take of this.

We finished our second Sunday in Seattle. I had scheduled for us to be in North Carolina two weeks after our time in Seattle. That would have given us two weeks to drive across the country. I wasn't expecting the problems with the motor home. With our flying from Seattle to Arkansas, our drive was actually going to be a lot shorter. We would fly out of Seattle on Monday morning and pick up our motor home in Arkansas on Monday afternoon. Tuesday morning, we could begin our drive to North Carolina. Everything was great. Well, maybe not. We arrived at the dealership in Arkansas on Monday afternoon. It was tough settling the account for the new engine, but God always provides. We spent the night in our motor home parked at the dealership. Early Tuesday morning, after a good breakfast, we pulled out. It had been good to be back in our rolling house, sleeping in our bed. It may be smaller than a real house, but it is home to us.

We were excited as we began the trip. We would be in a church in North Carolina, and from there we were headed to South Carolina. We'd been on the road for a while and were looking forward to being with family for the holidays.

The new engine sounded good when we cranked it up. It had three belts on it. We were seven miles down the road when all three belts came off. No. This couldn't be happening. Oh, yes, it could. They sent a tow truck to pull us back in. They put the belts back on and told us we were once again ready to go. It was late Thursday afternoon, but we could still get a ways down the road—maybe not. We didn't go far before the alternator burned up. How could the alternator be burning up? It was new. Once again, we were towed into the dealership. We ended up spending several nights in a motel.

We finally got back on the road. Between where we were in Arkansas and Memphis, Tennessee, I had to put the belts back on twice. I was able to do that myself. Why were they coming off? This was a new engine. We had to be towed again in Memphis when I noticed we were running a little bit hot. I wasn't about to damage the new engine by running it hot. The mechanic there told us there was a small leak in the radiator, as well as a transmission fluid leak, as well as an oil leak. This couldn't be good. The mechanic in Memphis just shook his head when he saw the new engine. He said, whoever worked on it before had things all messed up. He said he could get it where we could make it home, but we needed someone who knew what they were doing to repair it when we got home. As days were fleeting by, I had to do something I had never done before and would never do again in all the years we spent on the road. I had to cancel our meeting in North Carolina. Fortunately, it was not for a full week.

## WHERE ARE WE GOING TODAY, LORD?

We made it home on Wednesday, just in time to be with family for Thanksgiving on Thursday.

The motor home had done okay for the last leg of the trip from Memphis, so I thought (bad idea) I would drive it to the lower part of the state for one night so we could minister to some inmates in the state prison the next morning. We could then get our engine fixed properly. During the rest of the holiday season, we would be in local churches while we were finishing up our schedules for the new year. We spent the night in a grocery store parking lot.

Our daughter and son-in-law drove down early in the morning and met us at the prison. We went in together. It was nice having them with us. Things went well at the prison.

It was very cold that night as we were driving home. My son-in-law was with me in the motor home, and Lou Ellen was riding with our daughter behind us in case we had any trouble. We were on a lonely road in a wooded area. There were no other cars on the road besides us. We were only about fifty miles from home when I heard a loud noise, and the motor home began shaking. Something just happened, and I didn't know what. But something happened, and I knew it couldn't be good.

I pulled over on the side of the road. There wasn't much of a place to pull over. My daughter pulled over behind us, and she and Lou Ellen came running to us. They said something came flying up from behind us and almost hit her windshield. They found it on the side of the road. It was one of the fan blades from behind the radiator. How did that happen?

When the young man (I won't say mechanic) put the new water pump on the engine, he did not properly tighten the bolts. These are very long bolts. One of them came loose. And as it came out, it went into the fan, breaking off one of the blades. This caused the engine to vibrate as the fan was now unbalanced. I'd never heard of this happening, but now I was losing water around the gasket for the water pump. I needed this water to keep our new engine from overheating.

The last thing I wanted to do was to leave our motor home on this road late at night. It was pushing midnight. But if I tried to drive it, it would most likely run hot once the water leaked out. This was not good. Then I remembered I had about sixty gallons of water in my freshwater tank. This is used for bathing, cooking, etc. when you don't have a water hose hooked up. If I could just get the water into the radiator faster than it could leak out, we might be able to move our rolling house to a safer place.

We took the water hose we keep in the storage bin and stuck one end in the radiator. I had my son-in-law duct-tape it in place. I never traveled anywhere in our motor home without duct tape. I ran the other end of the hose into the window and over to the kitchen, where we attached it to the faucet. My son-in-law held it in place. I told him to turn the faucet on just as soon as I cranked the engine. It actually cranked. I immediately pulled out into the road and began driving. The missing fan blade caused us to vibrate terribly as we went down the road. I kept checking two gauges. One was the temperature gauge, and the other was the one telling me how much water we had left in our tank. About fifteen miles down the road, we came to a church. We pulled into the parking lot. The temperature gauge had been running a little higher than usual but not enough to do any damage to the engine. We still had about twenty gallons in the water tank. Something had told me I needed to make sure the tank was full, even though we wouldn't be using that much water. Thank You, Lord, for reminding me to fill up the water tank before we left on this trip.

I placed a note on the motor home, letting the people from the church know we had a tow truck coming. These towing bills were very expensive.

We had our regular mechanic pick it up the next day. He said he could not believe we had been able to drive it all, even before the fan blade incident. He had to take the engine out and start all over. (He had been NAPA mechanic of the year.) He found a wire attached to a bolt on one side of the engine that went to a screw on the other side of the engine. It wasn't doing anything. It was just there. He was amazed at how we had gotten off the road using a water hose and duct tape.

After the holidays were over, and the engine had been put in correctly, we were ready to travel again. But I remember the tow truck driver who picked us up on the side of the road in Arkansas when we originally broke down. He told me the people at the dealership were very good mechanics, who had a lot of experience and could replace motor home engines. The people at the dealership told me they were mechanics who could handle the job. They had certificates on the wall that said they were mechanics. Looking around the garage, they had all the tools and equipment that gave the *impression* they were mechanics. But their fruit said otherwise (Matthew 7:20).

# 4

## Priorities

### Luke 9:57–62

WE WOULD OFTEN do push-ups at Parris Island (marine corps boot camp). Our drill instructor would make us stay in the up position for long periods of time and then keep us in the down position for an extended period of time. Your arms would begin to shake as they were getting tired and you tried to keep yourself in the proper position. Your back was to be kept straight, and you'd better not let your belly touch the floor. As the sweat would drip to the floor from the tip of my nose, I'd try to see if I could make it land on the same spot each time. It helped to keep my mind off the agony of doing the push-ups.

One night, I looked over at my drill instructor and noticed something that changed the way I viewed him. I noticed he was not only doing push-ups with us but was doing one-arm push-ups, which was much more difficult than what we were doing. And when we put on a field marching pack, he had one on as well. He was not asking us to do anything he was not willing to do himself. In fact, he was actually doing much more. Not only had he been through boot camp when he first joined the marines but had been through drill instructor school, which was very difficult. He'd also served in combat in Vietnam. He was not asking me to do anything he was not doing himself. In fact, he had been through much more and was preparing me for what was to come.

Luke 9:57 says, "As they went." As they went where?—to Jerusalem. These words were spoken by Jesus as He was on His way to Jerusalem to make the ultimate sacrifice for us. He had "steadfastly set His face" toward Jerusalem. He is not asking too much of us; He has been through far more than He is asking of us.

In Luke 9:57, a man told Jesus, "I will follow You wherever You go". From Jesus's response, it seems Jesus knew that this man wasn't as committed as he sounded. He may have been a little more like John Mark, who quit the first time he went out on a mission for Christ (Acts 15:36–41).

A preacher went on a mission trip to India. Somehow, he had gotten the wrong idea of what it was going to be like. He thought he would be staying in a nice hotel during the day and preaching to large crowds in the evenings. Then he would return to the United States and tell everyone about all the people who came to know the Lord while he was preaching. He was not counting on wading through muddy rivers and pulling leeches off when he reached the other side. He wasn't counting on the food he would be eating or the lack of sleep or the difficult traveling conditions. He wanted to know if there was a way he could go home shortly after he arrived. He only thought he was committed to go on the trip. He was only committed to the idea of going and not actually going.

Jesus told the man in Luke 9:5 that He didn't have a place to stay at night. As a young lad, this verse upset me. I remember my Sunday school teacher reading this verse to us and telling us to think about it when we went to bed that night. She said, "When you lay your head on your pillow tonight, remember, Jesus had no pillow to lay His head on or no home to sleep in."

I felt so bad for Him. But that was not the purpose of what Jesus was saying. He wasn't wanting us to feel bad for Him. He wanted us to understand He had nothing holding Him back from His progress toward Jerusalem, where He would make the ultimate sacrifice for us.

Do we have anything holding us back when He calls us to salvation or to service? Do we have anything that is preventing our progress toward what His calling is for us? He told the rich man (Luke 18:22) to sell everything he had and give it to the poor. He didn't tell Abraham to sell everything and give it to the poor, even though he was rich. He didn't tell David to sell everything, even though he was wealthy. But he told the rich man in Luke 18 to do so because his wealth was the most important thing to him and was standing in the way of his service to the Lord.

# 5

## Mr. Slush

### Luke 9:57–62

BACK IN THE 1970s, we were serving as the minister of music and youth at a church. We went to every one of the local high school football games that year, even the away games, to support our youth and to mingle with the people in our community. One game, it was slushing—that is, a little bit of rain, a little bit of sleet, and a little bit of snow. It was cold and messy—really cold. I like to sit a ways up in the stands so I can see the plays developing on the field. As we sat down, we noticed one of the men from the church sitting several rows in front of us. It was a close game. The field was so messy from the weather; it was hard to read the numbers on the players' jerseys. They were covered in mud. The man from the church below us had a Totes umbrella he was trying to use to keep himself dry. It wasn't working. It was somewhat comical watching this grown man trying to stay dry under a small umbrella with the wind blowing. Everyone was wet and cold, but still hanging in, watching the game. Toward the end of the game, Mr. Slush (the nickname I gave him because of the game) got all excited when we took the lead with very little time left. He got so excited, he threw his little umbrella up in the air, stood up on the bleacher seats, and began to shout and scream with joy. He was a true fan. He was so excited. The cold, the wet, didn't seem to bother him as he cheered for his team. As the game ended, he ran onto the field, grabbing some of the players, hugging them, and getting mud all over himself from their uniforms. But that didn't matter; He was excited for his team. This win meant they were going to the state championship. As I was leaving and looking down on the field, I could see him all wet and muddy. But he didn't care, didn't bother him.

That was Friday night. Now it is Sunday morning, and we were sitting in church. It was during the gas and fuel shortage we endured in the 1970s. Some of you may remember waiting in the long lines to get gas, if you were able to find a station that had some. The preacher told us that it had been suggested that after the morning service, we turn the heat down real low in the church and bundle up for the evening service. (Back then, most churches had evening worship services, just like the morning service.) They said it would save a lot of fuel (many of the churches were using oil and natural gas for heat) if all the churches would do this. Immediately, guess who spoke up?—Mr. Slush. Mr. Slush pointed out that we, as a nation, were in a crisis. He seemed to like using the word *crisis* as he used it repeatedly. He ended by saying that we should only have our heat turned up high enough to prevent things from freezing so as to help in this crisis. However, he continued, it would be unheard of to expect people to come to church with very little heat, so he suggested we cancel the evening services.

Now I understand that there are those who can't sit in the sanctuary if we do not have the heat turned up. I'm beginning to deal with arthritis, and I know it doesn't go well with the cold. But as he was making his remarks, I kept picturing him up in the stands in the cold, wet, windy weather, cheering on his team, and the cold didn't seem to bother him. Could it be that he loved his football team so much that neither rain, sleet, or cold could keep him away from seeing them play? Not even the wet and mud on their uniforms kept him from hugging them. But now, he said, we could not expect anyone to come to a worship service for our Lord and Savior with a roof over our heads to keep the rain, sleet, and snow from falling on us and walls around us to keep the wind from blowing against us (better than a Totes umbrella). I know and understand that many would not be able to attend, but I had a little trouble with him not being able to attend after I watched him at that ball game. Could it be that he loved his high school football team more than he loved Jesus?—just asking. Could it be that his priorities were all messed up?

It is people like Mr. Slush that Jesus was referring to in these verses. Mr. Slush was using religious-sounding excuses for not being active for Christ. But Christ knows the difference.

# 6

## Can't Plow Looking Back

### Luke 9:62

I HAVE HEARD people talk about what they have given up to follow Jesus. "I used to be this or that, but I gave it all up to follow Jesus." To be completely honest with you, what have I given up?—nothing. Compared with what Christ has done, is doing, will do for me, anything I do for Him, anything I have given up, cannot measure up to what He has done.

He is preparing for me a home in heaven, and someday I will be there. I'm not worried about earthly treasure. "Follow Me," Jesus said.

Sometime back, while we were still on the road preaching revivals and conferences, I received a letter. It hurt. The writer told me I was forty-six years old (I was at that time) and had nothing. He said I was living on meager love offerings and living in an RV with no place to call home.

He didn't get it. I can sing "Amazing Grace," "Blessed Assurance," "What a Day That Will Be" because of what Christ has done. I can face tomorrow without fear because of Christ. There is nothing wrong with prosperity if that is where God puts you, but follow Him where He leads because that is where the joy is.

One evening, after being on the road several weeks straight, doing revivals, Lou Ellen and I were going out to dinner with some friends we hadn't seen in a while. Lou Ellen and I were sitting in the back seat. I was sitting right behind the driver. As we were headed down the bypass in Greenwood, the driver put his right arm on the back of his seat, twisted around, looked at me, and asked, "Where would y'all like to eat?"

I was a little nervous about him not looking where he was driving. I said, "It really doesn't matter. Where would y'all like to eat?"

He put his arm back up on the seat, turned toward me again, and asked, "Oh, I don't know. Where do you want to go?"

At that point, the car began to drift across the center line. Now I was more than a little nervous. His wife grabbed the wheel and turned the car back onto our side of the road. He didn't take too kindly to her taking the wheel. He slapped her hand (not too hard) and informed her that he was driving, and she was not to grab the wheel when he was driving. Then once again, his arm went back up on the seat as he asked, "Where would we like to eat?"

At this point, I was very nervous. I said, "I'm really hungry. There's a convenience store. let's just stop and get a Coke and some peanuts." I just wanted out. You can't drive looking back. You must focus on where you are going.

How do you make a straight row in a garden? At my first pastorate, I had several full-time farmers in my congregation. One Sunday morning, an elderly farmer in the church told me I could put more okra on a single row than anybody he'd ever seen. It made me feel good at first. But then he added, "But of course, your rows are more crooked than any rows I've ever seen." He then told me to be at his farm the next morning at 6:00 a.m. When I got there, he'd already prepared a spot of ground for us to use. He gave me a hoe. It was one that came to a point, not straight all the way across the blade. He told me to hold it behind my back so I could drag it behind me when I walked. He pointed to a stick he had driven into the ground on the other side of the prepared plot of ground and told me to walk toward the stick. He said, every time he asked me a question, I was to look back toward him while I answered the question as I continued walking toward the stick. Simple enough. I could do that. No problem. As I began to walk, he asked, "Nice day, don't you think?"

I turned my head toward him as I continued to walk and answered, "Yes, it is a nice day."

He asked, "Do you think it's going to rain?"

I answered, "It looks like it might."

As I finished walking toward the stick and answering questions, he said, "Now look at that line you made."

I said, "I see it. It looks just like the rows in my garden."

After enduring his picking at me, he said, "Now we are going to do it again," except this time I was not to take my eyes off the stick I was walking toward, even if a bolt of lightning was to hit between my legs. We raked out the crooked line I had made. Holding the hoe firmly with my hands behind my back, I locked my eyes on the stick across the garden. I began to walk. This time, when I responded to his questions and comments, I never took my eyes off the stick. Fortunately, there was not a single bolt of lightning. This time, the line was straight and true—well, almost. At one point, I hit a small rock, which knocked the hoe out of line, but it immediately corrected itself as I kept walking with my eyes on the goal.

I have laid my garden rows out this way ever since. We've got to learn to keep our eyes on Jesus and His plan for our lives and not become distracted by the things around us. Sure, we will hit a rock here and there, maybe get knocked off course. But as we keep our focus on Jesus and His word, we will stay on track.

# 7

## Jesus in the House

### Mark 2:1–12

I LOVE PREACHING overseas because in many places, the people are so eager to hear God's Word. I have preached in a house on a day when the temperature was over one hundred degrees. There was no air conditioner. The room would be empty of furniture so the people could all sit on the floor tightly squeezed next to each other. You could not see any portion of the floor as it was all covered by those sitting on it. We would stand at one end of the room and preach away. I can still hear the sound of the singing in such a crowded room. A crowd would form outside the door with people looking in because there was no more room to squeeze another person inside. There would be people gathered outside the window looking in. The heat, sweat, and crowded conditions didn't stop them from gathering. It was exhausting ministering in these conditions.

This is the scene I picture in this passage as Jesus was teaching at this house. The crowds had gathered, trying to see and hear Him. His presence in the house could not be concealed.

If Christ is in the house, that fact is going to be known. If Christ is in your heart, that fact is going to be known. *If* Christ is in your family, that fact is going to be known. And if Christ is in the church, that fact is going to be known.

You say, "Of course, He is in the church." I don't know. I don't know. Early in our ministry, I served as the minister of music and youth at a church for two years. During those two years, I worked under three preachers.

Lou Ellen and I had been working really hard to get a particular young man to come to church. We spent some time with him one Saturday and invited him to come to church. He told us he was going to come but couldn't come that week. He said he would be there the next week. We were excited that he was coming. The only problem (at least I thought it was the only problem. I didn't know a much bigger one was brewing) was that the preacher was going to be away on vacation, and I would be preaching. Lou Ellen would lead the congregational singing for me. The young man told us he wouldn't be there for the morning service but would definitely make it for the evening service. If he'd only come that morning.

When I arrived for the morning service, I noticed something in the bulletin that I hadn't seen when I looked at it before it was printed. Something had been added. At the bottom of the page was an announcement: "Everyone, be here tonight for a special called business meeting for the purpose of setting a termination date for our pastor."

Before the pastor left for his vacation, he told me that he may get back sometime Sunday afternoon, but he and his wife would visit another church that night. If I saw his car in the driveway at the parsonage, I was not to think I wasn't still preaching. On their way in, they pulled into the church parking lot, and he asked his wife to run in and pick up a bulletin in case there was something he might need to know. Oh, there was something he needed to know. He was thinking someone might be in the hospital that he might need to check on. He was an excellent pastor.

When his wife returned, and he was driving off, he asked if she saw anything. She said, "I think you need to read this."

That night, there was a lot of talking going on as people were entering the church. The Sunday night crowd was going to be much bigger than usual. Just before the service began, the young man we had been trying to get to come to church came walking in. As he entered, he told the ushers he knew Lou Ellen and me, so they brought him to the front and asked him if he would like to sing in the choir. He said, "Yes." He now had a ringside seat for what was about to take place, and it is not going to be worship. I had wanted him to come, but now that he was here, I was a bit uncertain about it being this particular night.

Everyone was in shock when the pastor and his wife came walking in, as if it was a normal Sunday evening. He had called me that afternoon and told me that he felt led to come back early from his vacation and that I could preach the message I had prepared another time. I didn't ask any questions. At that point, I knew that he had seen the bulletin or someone had called him.

I wasn't sure how things were going to go. I was prepared to lead the hymns and choir anthem. The pastor asked me to come and lead the church in a hymn. As I stood up, the chairman of the deacons told me to sit back down because we had a matter of business to take care of. As I was sitting down, the pastor said that the meeting was out of order, according to parliamentary procedure and our church constitution and bylaws. (The pastor was right.) I was told to stand and lead the hymn. The chairman of the deacons once again told me to sit down so we could handle this business. I was raised to follow instructions. I was in the marine reserves, so I understood orders. But I couldn't follow two opposing orders at the same time. I'm not that good. Would we sing or not?

As you can imagine, things got rather ugly. When the service (can't really call it a service) was over, and the dust settled, I was standing down front when the young man came down with a big smile on his face. I was embarrassed and began to apologize. He stopped me and said he wanted to apologize to me. He said, "Why didn't you tell me it was like this? I pay a lot of money to go to the auditorium to see a fight. This is one of the best ones I've ever seen, and it didn't cost me a penny."

We may laugh at that. But here was a man needing Jesus, wanting to see Jesus, trying to see Jesus, but he didn't see Jesus that night even though he went to church.

Is Jesus in your house?

# 8

## No Need for a Sign

### Mark 2:1–12

BACK IN THE 1990s, we were taking part in a missions conference in North Carolina. At one of the evening services, the choir from the church I was pastoring in South Carolina (didn't go into full-time evangelism and missions until 1998) was going to sing right before I brought the closing message for the night. I was touched they would make the two-hour drive to be there after they got off work and would then have to make the drive back after the services.

Our kids were staying with me in North Carolina as there were a lot of activities for them at the conference. However, my wife had to stay home that week. I was not used to her not being with me. She would usually travel with me and would sing and take part in the conferences.

The choir arrived just as the service was starting, so I didn't get to speak to my wife before she went up into the choir loft. A soloist sang before the first preacher preached. I was sitting on the front row of the congregation, ready to go up into the pulpit after the choir sang. My wife was in the front row of the choir. They did a great job. We were all blessed by the message in the song. As I went up, the choir was coming down. They came across the platform and down the steps into the congregation. I stood there, nodding to them as they went by. But as my wife came by, I gave her a hug. I hadn't seen her all week, and I was glad to see her. Then I thought, *I hope they realize this is my wife, and I didn't just pick one out as they came walking by.*

But I noticed something about my wife. She was wearing my favorite perfume—well, not my perfume but her perfume that I like for her to wear.

How did I know she was wearing that particular perfume? Was it because while she was sitting in the choir, she was holding a sign that read, "Honey, I'm wearing the perfume you like"? No! Was it because, when I hugged her, she whispered in my ear, "Honey, I'm wearing your favorite perfume"? No! Was it because I saw the droplets running down her wrists, neck, and behind her ears, where y'all put it?

No! I perceived it was there. I smelled it. I knew it was there without her holding up a sign or telling me.

If Jesus is in your house, your heart, your family, your church, that fact will be known, and you don't have to run around telling everyone you are a Christian; people will know.

# 9

## Are We Really Friendly?

### First Peter 4:8–10

WE HAD JUST finished a revival in Arkansas and were to go the next Sunday to Missouri for a one-day revival. We left our RV in Arkansas and got up early Sunday morning for the drive to Missouri. The pastor of the church we were going to had told me his was the friendliest church in Missouri. Not only that, he also told us they served a full breakfast every Sunday morning. I was already liking this church.

We got up at five that morning and began the drive. When we arrived at the church, the snow had begun to lightly cover the ground. As I was getting out of our truck, a young lady was getting out of the car beside us. I said, "Good morning!" She said nothing as she got out and began to hurry to one of the entrances to the church. I figured she either didn't hear me (which was unlikely because I have a loud voice), she was cold and wanted to hurry inside, or she was hungry and wanted to get to breakfast. What I know is that she didn't speak or even acknowledge us with a nod.

As we entered the building, not a single person spoke to us. There were people going in every direction, but not one of them welcomed us or asked if we needed any help finding anything. I know we had been up for a while, but surely, in this cold weather, my deodorant hadn't worn off that fast. Then I recognized the smell of bacon. I knew which way to go.

We entered the fellowship hall and went over to the food line. I picked up a tray, silverware, and some napkins and started down the line. As I did, a lady, without looking up at me, said, "Bacon or sausage?"

Normally, I would have said both, but not today. I didn't want to upset her. When we left the line, we sat down at one of the round tables. Round tables are designed for fellowship. Everyone can easily see each other, and all can participate in the conversation. But no one sat down with us. We were alone in a room quickly filling up with people.

I couldn't help but notice how friendly they were with each other, just not with someone new. As we were eating, the pastor came in. I had talked with him over the phone but had never met him in person. He came over to our table and said, "You must be the Osteens?"

I said, "Yes."

He then announced to everyone who we were. Now everyone wanted to talk with us.

After the evening service, we were getting ready to begin our drive back to our RV in Arkansas. The pastor, with a big smile on his face, said, "Didn't I tell you we had the friendliest church in Missouri?"

I answered, "Yes."

That is what he told me. But he didn't leave it there. He went on to ask, "Well, I was right, wasn't I?"

I answered, "I hope not. If we hadn't been preaching and singing, we may have left and gone to another one of the churches in the area." I wasn't trying to be smart but wanted to help them reach even more people than they were. I went on to explain how friendly they were with each other but not with us before they knew who we were. Someone new would feel uncomfortable not knowing where to go or what to do, especially in a large church. I went on to praise the church for all the things they were doing well but encouraged them to make a special effort to reach out to those who may not have come with one of their regular members.

We crossed the state line into Arkansas near midnight. As we crossed the line, we topped a hill, and the speed limit suddenly dropped. Sitting on the other side of the speed limit sign was a policeman. Yep, I got a ticket. It was still a good day of worship and service to our Lord and Savior.

# 10

## Effort Required

Nehemiah 1:3–4; 2:2–5, 18

I TOOK MY first church staff position at the beginning of my sophomore year at Anderson Junior College in Anderson, South Carolina. (It is Anderson University now.) I was a music major, preparing to become a minister of music. There was a notice on the bulletin board in the music department for a part-time music director at a small rural church. They paid ten dollars a week. Duties would include leading the worship service on Sunday mornings and conducting choir practice on Wednesday nights. While I would not make anything, it would give me experience, and most importantly, it would give me the opportunity to share the gospel.

Lou Ellen and I had been dating for about six months when we made our first drive to the church. It was about thirty minutes from the college, where I picked Lou Ellen up. I was still living at home, so I had already driven about forty minutes from Greenville.

We met with the committee, had a brief choir rehearsal during the Sunday school hour, and led the music for the worship service. I felt like things were going well, until that second hymn. I don't remember the name of the hymn we were singing, but I will never forget what happened. I felt I was doing a good job hiding how nervous I was. I had never done anything like this before. I had always found it difficult standing before a group of people. I had my arms going in just the right pattern as I was leading the hymn. It later became second nature, but I was a beginner at this point. In fact, I'd never led congregational singing before, except for class. I had sat under a lot of great directors in the church youth choir, high school chorus, All-State Chorus, Greenville Singing Christmas Tree. I had learned a lot from them as to how it should be done. But there is a big difference when it comes to doing it yourself. I was holding the hymnbook with my left hand and leading with my right. (I later didn't hold the hymnal so I would have both hands free.) As my right hand was coming across my body, marking the second beat of the measure, it caught the bottom of the hymnbook, sending it flying out of my hand. I'm really not sure how I managed to do that, but I did. It was pretty embarrassing, especially when I was trying to get a job. I was standing on the edge of the platform, so it didn't simply fall next to my feet. That would have been too easy to recover from. It fell onto the floor in front of the platform. I had to step down from the platform, pick up the hymnal, get back on the platform, and find the page. I felt my face turning red. When I got back into position and found the page, the hymn was over. I figured there was no way I would get the job. At least things had gone really well with the choir.

To my amazement, they called me as their minister of music for $10 a week. After I had been there a month, someone stood up in a business meeting and made the motion they would double my salary. It now covered my gas expenses.

Serving the Lord through that church was a special time for us as we grew in our faith and experience. They loved us and were patient with us as we were learning. I learned that I must pray, put forth the effort to do what the Lord was calling me to do and go where He was leading me to go, believing that where my abilities end, He will step in.

I loved my mother-in-law. We seemed to hit it off the first time we met. She treated me like a son. I would do whatever I could to help her. I always felt that she loved me too. But on one occasion, it seemed she was trying to get rid of me, even though she was trying to help.

## WHERE ARE WE GOING TODAY, LORD?

Every year, the last weekend in August, Williamston, South Carolina, has what they call the Spring Water Festival. My wife, Lou Ellen, grew up there, and that's where her parents still lived. There is a mineral spring that comes up from the ground in the park, and people from all around come to get water. It's actually very good water. During the festival, booths are set up all over the park with crafts, food, etc. It usually draws a pretty good crowd.

One of the activities is the spring water run. I have been a runner most of my life and thought I might enter. I didn't have any expectations of winning my age category but thought it would be fun to enter. The only problem was that I hadn't been running for about a year. This would give me something to train for. Before I signed up, I wanted to find out just how long was the run and when the festival was going to be. At that time, I didn't know the regular date for the festival. I called my mother-in-law and asked if she could find out when the festival was and how far I would have to run. She said she would get back with me in a couple of days.

She was all excited when she called me back on a Monday night. She not only told me it was a four-mile run but also told me the route. This concerned me because I knew there would be some serious hills to run for someone who hadn't been running for a while. I figured, if I had enough time and trained hard, I might be able to get back in shape enough to enter. There was a time I'd run ten miles at a time so I could work my way back up to four. But then she told me it was the next Saturday. That was less than a week. At that point, any plans I had to enter the run went out the window. There was no way I could get ready for a four-mile run with only about four days to train. It was not going to happen this year. Before I had a chance to tell her I would have to wait, she told me that she had told her Sunday school class that her son-in-law was going to be running in the spring water run and that many of them had said they would come out to watch. She seemed so excited about everything, but I was not. I was thinking, *This is not going to happen.* Then she told me she had already registered me and paid my entrance fee so I wouldn't have to worry about trying to do so in such a short period of time. That's not what I was concerned about. I was concerned about grasping for air while trying to run up a hill. She went on to explain that all I needed to do was pick up my packet and my number to pin onto my shirt when I arrived. I would even get a commemorative T-shirt in my packet.

She was so excited and had put so much effort on my behalf. How could I tell her I wasn't going to run? I didn't want her to have to go back and tell her friends I wasn't going to run after she had said I was. I tried to express excitement as I thanked her for all she had done. Maybe there would be a lightning storm or something, and they would have to cancel the race.

There weren't any storms, and the run went on as scheduled. I did what little preparation I could on Tuesday, Wednesday, and Thursday, mostly stretching and short easy runs to get loosened up so I wouldn't have any major muscle cramps or pulls. A few years back, I could run ten miles. But now I didn't know if I could run one mile without stopping and waiting for my oxygen to catch up with me.

At eight o'clock, Saturday morning, all the runners gathered behind a line drawn across Main Street in front of McDonald's. I'm not sure how it happened, but I was on the front row with my toes just behind the starting line. (These spots are usually reserved for the more elite runners.) As we got ready to start, Miss Williamston or Miss Spring Water Festival Queen took a starter pistol (shoots only blanks for starting races) and pointed it up into the air. I hadn't been this nervous since my days of starting a race on my high school track team. She pulled the trigger, and the race was on. For a moment, a very brief moment, I was in front of everyone. I have always had quick reflexes, and at the sound of the gun, I was on my way. Okay, I was only in front for one stride, and then the others at the front of the pack began to pass by me. I was amazed at how well I was doing until about the two-mile mark. I was running somewhere in the middle of the pack. I had settled into my stride and thought, *I'm going to finish this thing. Not very fast, but I'm going to finish.* I could hear the sound of someone coming up behind me. I figured it must be a kid by the sound of their shoes hitting the pavement. I expected to be passed by those in the younger categories. (I was in my earlier forties.) Then they came up beside me. It was an older woman, a senior citizen, and she went by me without any effort. She wasn't even breathing hard. As she went by, she looked at me with a grin on her face and said, "Good morning. Beautiful day, isn't it?"

Trying not to show I was struggling, I said, "Yes, ma'am, sure is. Great day for a run." And then she was gone. I found out, after the race, she was sixty-nine years old and ran in races all the time. I could tell she loved running past the younger folks. I finished the race but was sore for several days. I have continued to run from that day forward. I am seventy and still running several miles a day.

I was reminded from that experience that bold goals are only going to be reached by bold effort. I had a goal. That goal was to once again be able to run for several miles at a time. I prayed that I would get back into shape, but I had to put forth the effort.

We come to church and talk about reaching people for Christ. We pray about reaching people for Christ, but it will not happen if we do not move past the talking and praying and get to work. God will hear our prayers and help us and guide us, but we must put forth the effort.

Nehemiah 4:6 says, "We built the wall." They had a willingness to get busy and do whatever was necessary to be done, even when it was hard and difficult. They worked together for God's glory and not their own.

# 11

## Run Baby Run

### John 3:16

ONE AFTERNOON, WHEN Lou Ellen and I were still newlyweds, we were walking in a pasture with our trusty companion, Bullet (our bird dog). We enjoyed walking together and dreaming about what the Lord may have in store for us. We had no idea what He was preparing.

As we were walking, we saw a pair of foxes walking in the pasture as well. It surprised me to see them walking out in the open.

Bullet saw them about the same time we did. His eyes locked on them as their eyes locked on us. Bullet immediately took off running toward them as fast as he could.

The smaller of the two foxes lay down in the tall grass, and we could no longer see it. But the slightly larger one took two or three strides toward Bullet and then made a hard right and took off as fast as he could. Bullet took the bait and took off behind him. The chase was on. The fox stayed just ahead of Bullet making sure he didn't catch him but also that he didn't fall too far behind.

As we were watching the chase, we noticed the smaller fox stood up and headed in the opposite direction. She wasn't moving very fast. She came to a small opening at the bottom of the fence and squeezed through. She crossed the road and went to the edge of the woods on the other side. She then turned around and lay back down looking back toward the pasture. I realized what was going on. The smaller fox was female and was pregnant.

I returned my attention back to the chase going on in the pasture. The fox was making a giant circle in the pasture with Bullet on his heels. He was circling back to where it had all started. As he saw his mate, he suddenly turned toward the hole in the fence and put his legs in high gear increasing the distance between himself and Bullet. Bullet was fast but not as fast as a fox.

He shot through the opening in the fence and darted across the road. Bullet crashed into the fence as he tried to fit through the small opening. It wasn't happening, so he began to dig furiously trying to dig under the fence. As the fox came through the fence and crossed the street, its mate stood up, and they leisurely walked into the woods together. Bullet was still digging.

I called Bullet, and he immediately came running back to me and Lou Ellen. It had been an exciting walk—an exciting run for Bullet. But as we walked, we were talking about how the male fox, without any hesitation, had risked his life for his mate and unborn children. I couldn't help but think about what Christ had done for us. He not only risked His life but actually died for us in a horrible way. He gave His life to pay the price for our sins. It gets even better that He rose again so that we could live with Him for all eternity as long as we put our faith and trust in Him as our Lord and Savior.

How can we not love Christ, and how can we not live for Him?

# 12

## Workers Together

### Second Corinthians 6:1–6; First Corinthians 12:1–4

WE GENERALLY GO to India during their dry season. One, we are able to minister without dealing with all the rain and mud. It would be difficult to travel and conduct outdoor services. It is also a cooler weather. I have been there in April and May when the temperature was well over one hundred degrees. This is rough when there is no air-conditioning.

One year, in January or February, they were having weather conditions influenced by an El Niño. This changed normal weather patterns, and something happened that I was not used to seeing in India. It rained. As a result, the next morning, the roads were muddy and difficult to travel. We were traveling with several people in the car—no seat belts here. Suddenly, the car bogged down and sank into the mud. We weren't just stuck; we were stuck stuck. Another car was behind us with even more people in it. It's amazing how many people pack into a car. It stopped before it got stuck. They carefully got me out of the car, making sure I didn't get muddy. I didn't mind getting dirty and was ready to help dig this car out. But as their quest, they wanted to take care of me and insisted I let them do it. My dear Indian friend and translator stood next to me on a hill, overlooking the situation as all the men jumped in and started to free the car. I chuckled when I saw the problem. They weren't getting anywhere. My translator said, "No worry, they get it out." Then he saw the problem. There were several young men standing in the mud, pushing the rear of the car forward as the driver tried to drive it out. The wheels would spin and throw mud back on the young men, but they would not quit pushing. There was not a lack of effort or desire to help, even in all the mud. At the same time, there was a couple of young men at the front of the car, pushing backward. They were working against each other. Quickly realizing what they were doing, they all began to push and pull in the same direction (it's called working together), and the car came out of the mud. We had a good laugh as we loaded back into the cars. However, all their efforts to keep the mud off me went down the drain when we sat together in the car. But that was no problem.

We have a lot of churches with people who are working hard, yet they are not reaching people for Christ. So often, the problem is that they are not working together. They don't have a unified vision or mission statement. Each person, committee, or group is just out there, doing their own thing and not working with others. Of course, there's also the problem with those who just don't do anything. They expect the church to have all the ministries and programs to benefit them and their family, but they have no desire to take part and do what they can to help. It's their loss.

A lady came forward during an invitation and told me the Lord was leading her to take a more active role in the church. She wanted to "do something," she said. I asked her what she felt led to do. She said she wasn't sure. I told her we needed someone to help on the hostess committee. She immediately told me she didn't want anything to do with the kitchen or preparing meals. She said, "Is there something else I could do?"

I said we needed another person on our nursery rotation. She would only have to help during Sunday school or worship every fourth or fifth week.

She said, "No, I don't want to take care of any babies or little children."

I reminded her that we were having a clean-up day the next Saturday, and she could come and simply join in wherever she wanted and stay only as long as she wanted. She could help inside or outside, whichever she chose. She said, no, that wasn't for her. "Not what I had in mind."

I suggested she come back when she was ready to serve.

I heard one preacher put it this way: "The reason why some churches prosper and others do not is because, in some churches, everybody is involved doing what they can."

It is time we fall in love with Jesus. We can identify what needs to be done and have meetings to come up with a plan. We can pray about it. But until we work together and put forth some effort, nothing will happen.

# 13

## The Call of an Older Man

### Exodus 3:1–12; 2:23–25

ONE SUNDAY MORNING, as I was turning forty, I really wasn't thinking about my age. It has never bothered me. As I was getting dressed for church, I noticed both my kids, as well as my wife, were wearing black. I didn't think anything of it, so I put my black suit on. When I got to church, I knew something was off. It just didn't feel right. There was something in the air. It didn't take long for me to notice that everyone came to church dressed in black. For the past two weeks, in the hallways and Sunday school classes, they were telling everyone that on this particular Sunday, everyone was to wear black in honor of their pastor's fortieth birthday. I fit right in, wearing my black suit. My wife and kids said they had a hard time keeping a straight face when they saw me in my black suit.

I couldn't help but chuckle when I looked across the congregation from the pulpit. They loved their pastor, and I loved them.

The next day, I was jogging, when a lady from the church drove up beside me. She slowed down, rolled down her window, and told me I'd better stop running and get into her car and let her take me back to the parsonage. I was puzzled as to why she was saying this. As I continued to run, I told her I was fine. But she said, "No, you're not. You just turned forty, so you can't do things like this anymore."

Moses was twice forty when God called on him to lead His people out of Egypt. Don't ever think that you can't do anything for the Lord as you get older. David was only a teenager when God used him to take on and defeat Goliath. Gideon was a little older. You may not be able to do the same things as you get older, but God still has a plan for you, one in which He has been preparing you for.

Moses spent the first forty years of his life growing up and serving in Pharaoh's court. He received the best training and education available at that time. He learned the proper protocol for approaching the king and his court, which is what he would later be called upon to do when the time came for him to lead God's people out of Egypt. He spent the next forty years of his life living in the desert as a shepherd. He learned the ways of desert living. This is the same area where he would be leading God's people. Now at eighty, Moses was ready for what God had been preparing him for. He had no idea what God was preparing him to do.

# 14

## Wake Up!

### Romans 13:11–14

ROMANS 13:11 TELLS us it is "high time to wake up." That means it is getting late, and we need to get moving. Almost every alarm clock, even the ones we have on our phones, has a snooze button. This way, when it goes off, we can hit it and keep sleeping for a bit longer. The alarms used to be loud ringing bells or a terrible buzzer sound that would wake you quickly, but not now. We can't have that. We have gentle sounds. Some start soft and slowly get louder. I have reveille on my phone to wake me up. But I once read about an electric car alarm clock. It made a loud noise when it went off. You set it on the floor next to your bed after you set the time for it to go off. When it went off, it wouldn't just make a terrible loud sound; it would also take off across the floor. If it hit something, like a wall or piece of furniture, it would simply spin around and go in the other direction. There was no snooze button. In order to turn it off, you had to get up and chase it down. By the time you caught it, you were wide awake. I imagine a lot of them had a short life as they were thrown once they were caught. My kids heard me talking about these and gave me one. I haven't broken it yet.

Paul believed the Lord was coming back soon and had an urgency for serving Him. That is something we are lacking today.

## JIM OSTEEN

We need to wake up. He may very well come back in our lifetime. If He doesn't, we only have so much time here, and we need to make sure we are ready and using our time well.

# 15

## Oh No, I'm Being Tempted

### First Corinthians 10:12–13

HAVE YOU EVER been tempted? That's what I thought. We have to keep in mind that it is not a sin to be tempted. We sin when we give in to the temptation. I love this verse: "But God is faithful, Who will not allow you to be tempted beyond what you are able."

I call the time between Thanksgiving and New Year's "eating season." With all the family and church dinners, there will be a lot of feasting and very little fasting.

As I got on the elevator at one church, I checked the weight limit. It had a weight limit of 2,500 pounds. That meant I could enjoy all the holiday meals and still ride the elevator.

Many years back, we were going through the mountains of Arkansas. The cell phone we had at the time didn't have GPS. The motor home we had at that time didn't have a backup camera. (I know this is hard for some of our younger folks to imagine.) We had a set of walkie-talkies that we used in some places. Lou Ellen would stand at the back of the RV and direct me when I was backing around corners or in tight spots. We came to the road we were to turn on. I wasn't sure about this. It was a winding road, winding down into a deep valley. It really wasn't much of a road. But once I started, there was no place I could turn the motor home around. I was being careful not to burn up the brakes going down the hill. The further down into the valley we went, the more concerned I became. It would be difficult to try to back our way back out. It was also beginning to get dark. Finally, we reached the bottom of the hill, where we came to a little wooden bridge with no side rails. It was just wide enough for us to cross. I wasn't worried about staying on the bridge. If it was wide enough, I could drive over it. But I wasn't sure the old wooden bridge could bear the weight of our motor home with all that we had in it. I pulled up to the bridge, got out, lay on the ground, and began to inspect underneath the bridge. I saw that there were some large beams underneath that would support us. Since I was already on my knees, I said a prayer, thanking God for the bridge and asking Him to strengthen the bridge and lighten our RV. I prayed we would not only get over the bridge but also get up to the other side of the valley without getting a running start. We made it and eventually came to an open area, where the church was. We ended up going there several times. The Lord always blessed.

I knew elevators, bridges, and other things have their limits. God is telling us that we are not going to be tempted beyond our limit, beyond what we are able to bear. That's why, when I find myself being tempted, I remember that I will not be tempted more than what I can handle if I stay true to His word.

# 16

## Can You Hear Me Now?

### Isaiah 59:1–2

AT ONE CHURCH, I served as pastor before we went into missions and evangelism. We had two very elderly ladies. They were just as sweet as they could be, but their hearing was about gone. They could not come every week because of their health. I was always glad to see their smiling faces and to chat with them. But occasionally, they would both show up on the same Sunday. They would sit together, which was not always good. They would take their place on the second row, just to my left, as I would be in the pulpit. They would try to talk to each other. They thought they were whispering, but just about everyone in the church could hear them.

"What did he say?"

"I think he said…"

The people of Isaiah's day were wondering if this had happened to God. Had He lost His strength? Was He no longer able to hear their prayers? In Isaiah 59:2, we get the answer. Isaiah told them God had not lost His power or His ability to hear. He told them the problem was with them: It was their sin.

Back when Lou Ellen and I were in our twenties, we were serving as temporary house parents for a youth home for status offenders. The girls' room was on one end of the hall, and the guys' rooms were on the other end of the hall. We had a suite in the middle of the hall.

Mandy, our newborn daughter, was in a crib right next to our bed, so Lou Ellen could simply reach over and pick her up if need be. We also let Bullet, our bird dog, stay in our room at night. If anyone should forget which end of the hall they were supposed to be on and started drifting to the other end, Bullet would let us know.

Things had been going so well, until in the middle of one night, chaos broke loose. Everyone, the girls, the boys, as well as us were sleeping so well when it happened. All of a sudden, we were awakened when Bullet began barking. Then Lou Ellen let out a scream as something ran across our bed. Then here came Bullet across our bed, right behind it. Lou Ellen, with a mother's instinct, reached over and cradled Mandy in her arms to protect her. It was dark, and we had no idea what was happening or what had just run across our bed. What we did know was that Bullet wanted it. The children didn't have any idea what was going on either. They just heard the sound of a dog barking and howling, a baby crying, and the sound of furniture being turned over and things falling to the floor.

Bullet was all over the place. I turned the lights on, just in time to see it. It was a squirrel, and Bullet was right behind it. Somehow, a squirrel had gotten into the house and picked the wrong room. Bullet was determined to catch it. Can you imagine a squirrel and a hunting dog in a room together?—not good.

The squirrel, in an attempt to evade the dog, jumped onto the dresser, ran across to the other side, and then jumped off. That might work for a squirrel. But when Bullet jumped onto the dresser, his momentum let him slide all the way across to the other side, knocking over everything that was on the dresser. By now all the kids were up and outside our locked door.

Keep in mind that the kids could only hear what was going on and not see what was actually happening. Most of them had come from bad home situations, where they were used to Mom and Dad getting into fights. They were banging on the door, thinking we were really getting into it. We couldn't open the door because we wanted to keep the squirrel contained in our room and not carry the chase and destruction to other parts of the house. The squirrel ran under the coffee table with no problem. It made it just fine. Bullet tried to follow it under the coffee table—big problem. When Bullet lowered his head and tried to run under it, it turned over. I grabbed a blanket and threw it over the squirrel as it went by. We had him. Bullet was having a fit, trying to get into that blanket. He had chased that squirrel too long not to get to it.

It was all over in a matter of a few minutes. But the room was a disaster. We let the kids in so they could see what had actually happened. I could feel the squirrel's heart beating fast as I held it in the blanket. I uncovered his head so the kids could touch its head. I even let Bullet get a look and a sniff of it. It helped to calm him down. We took the squirrel outside and let him go, where I imagine he went and told all the other squirrels they had better avoid going into that house.

I have to admit, it was a bit comical after it was all over. As we were cleaning up the mess, the children told us of all the different things they thought were happening. We learned a lot about these children that night, which helped us as we ministered to them. Of all the things they thought were going on, no one thought a squirrel might be in the room. It wasn't the baby. It wasn't the dog. It wasn't Lou Ellen. It wasn't me causing all the trouble and disturbance. It was the squirrel.

Isaiah told the people to put the blame where it belonged. It wasn't that God's arm had been shortened (that He'd lost His strength) or that He had lost His hearing. It was their sin. Jesus spoke about this in Matthew 3:25: "Woe unto you Scribes and Pharisees, hypocrites! for you make clean the outside of the cup and dish, but inside they are full of extortion and self-indulgence."

# 17

## Not Hidden to Him

### Proverbs 15:3

AS A KID, I would often go to my uncle's farm. He had several horses.

One day, I was riding Delightful Surprise. She was a well-trained Tennessee walking horse. We were going down a trail through the woods. We were about half a mile from the barn. Suddenly, Delightful stopped. I said, "Let's go." She didn't budge. I gently tapped her, but she didn't move. This was unusual for her as it normally took so little to get her to go where you wanted her to go. This was a show horse with many ribbons to her credit. I spoke louder and gently kicked her with my heels. She didn't move.

I was starting to get a little agitated with her. I kicked her harder and tapped her with a crop. Still she didn't move. After a few moments of this, I knew something must be wrong, so I started to get off to check her feet. As I leaned forward to get off, she threw her head back, hitting me and knocking me back up into the saddle. She did this twice. Now at this point, I was both mad and confused. For some reason, she didn't want to move, nor did she want me to get off her back. Something must really be going on. As I once again started to get off, putting my hand on the back of her neck so she couldn't sling her head back, and I could quickly throw my leg over her to get off, she started to slowly step backward.

## WHERE ARE WE GOING TODAY, LORD?

It was at this point that I noticed something coming out of the bush and quickly crossing the trail. Now it all made sense. It was a copperhead snake. She knew the snake was there, even though I didn't. She was not going to walk by it and get bitten, nor was she going to let me get off her, where I might get bitten.

Sometimes we don't know what we are asking. We don't know what lies ahead, but the Lord does. Maybe we ought to listen to Him.

# 18

## Where's the Fire

### Romans 8:1

ONE NIGHT, BACK in the 1960s, when I was just a kid, a friend of mine, who lived up the street, and I were sleeping in a tent in our backyard. We were roughing it. We had a long extension cord pulled from my parents' bedroom window to a portable TV in the tent. We had aluminum foil wrapped on the rabbit ears for good reception. (Those of you from the sixties will remember the rabbit ear antennas and the aluminum foil.)

Early in the morning, just a little before sunrise, another guy, a little older than us, came to our tent and woke us up. He asked if we wanted to have some fun. We followed him down the street to a utility pole, which had a fire alarm on it (common in those days before cell phones). All you had to do was pull it, and it would sound off at the fire station, and the fire trucks would be on the way.

No way was I going to pull it with no fire in sight. I knew such an act would bring severe consequences from my dad. The older kid explained how it worked and how we could get away with pulling the alarm and getting to see the fire trucks as well. No, I was not going to have part of pulling that fire alarm, no chance I was going to do it. He said, "Well, at least touch it." That I could do. I put my fingers on the little pull-down bar. My friend put his fingers on top of mine, and then the big kid put his on top and pulled down hard. It immediately began making a clanging noise. I wanted to run. Everything within me said, "*Run!*" But he said, "No, it would make us look guilty. Just calmly walk down the street, as if nothing is happening."

As we began to walk down the street, I could hear the fire truck sirens. First, a police car came rushing by, then the red fire chief's car. Next came two shiny red fire trucks. They were followed by another police car. As each one raced by, we continued walking, not even looking at them. It amazed me how fast they had responded and gotten there.

We walked into Dunkin' Donuts on 291 Bypass. I believe it was the first Dunkin' Donut shop to open in Greenville, South Carolina. It's not at that location anymore. We took our place on some stools at the counter. People were coming in for their coffee and donuts before going to work.

Then the fire chief showed up. My heart sank when I saw his car pulling up. I still remember those big red suspenders holding his fire uniform pants up. His face was as red as his suspenders. It was obvious he was not happy. He came straight for us. He said he knew there was not a fire as soon as he saw us walking away from where the fire trucks were going instead of running to see them. He gave us a lecture on what would happen if a real fire broke out somewhere else, and they were here. Everyone in the place was staring at us as he lectured us. I just sat there, not admitting or denying anything. I was thinking this was not going to end well. It was not the fun he said we would have. I was embarrassed as I felt the stares of the people all around us. He got our names and told us he was going to call our parents.

We walked back to the house. The big kid dropped off at his house. My dad was in the yard. The sirens had woken him up. He figured we were out chasing the fire trucks. I told Dad we did get to see the fire trucks but that there was not a real fire. It had been a false alarm. He asked if we'd seen or talked to any of the firemen. (He knew several of them, including the chief.) I told him yes and that they thought we had pulled the fire alarm. At that point, my dad's demeanor changed. He looked at me and asked, "Did you do it?"

I was not going to lie to him. I said, "Yes, we pulled it." I went on to explain what had happened. My dad looked at my friend and told him he was to go home and tell his dad what had happened before he called him himself. Then Dad took me inside. This was not going to be good. The big kid said we were going to have fun; this was not going to be fun.

Dad, after telling my mom and sister (my sister was three years older than me) what had happened, told me to head for the bedroom. I knew what was coming. As I walked down the hall to the bedroom, I was a man under condemnation. I had done the deed, been found guilty, and now was waiting for the punishment to be carried out. For me, it would not be a long wait, just like a man on death row, who is said to be condemned. That's because he is under condemnation. He has done the crime, been found guilty, and is waiting for the sentence to be carried out.

It was a quiet walk as we walked down the short hallway to the bedroom. My dad was walking behind me. I felt so bad, not because I'd gotten caught and was about to be punished but because of what I'd done when I knew better. I put myself in this position and hurt my parents in doing so.

As we entered the bedroom, I heard the sound of Dad's belt sliding through the belt loops as he was removing it from his waist. I was never beaten or abused, but there were a few times when Dad got my attention when I'd done something really bad. I lay across the bed on my stomach. Okay, here it came.

But then, something happened I was not expecting. My dad lay across the bed beside me, looking in my direction. I turned my head toward his. He handed me the belt. He said, "Take it." I wasn't sure what was happening, but maybe this was not going to be as bad as I thought. As I took the belt, he told me to stand up. I did. He continued to lay across the bed. As he lay there, he said, "Lay it on me." I just stood there, really confused. He repeated the words, "Lay it on me." He said, "I'm going to do for you what Jesus did for us on the cross when He paid the price for our sins." I think it would have been easier for me if he'd gone ahead and given me the spanking.

I took the belt and, with tears of love for my dad running down my face, hit him as gently as I could. He probably barely felt the belt touching him. After one or two touches, he gave me a big bear hug, sat me down beside him, and we had a good talk. We talked not only just about what I had done but also about what Christ had done for us and the pain He received.

On that morning, my dad impressed upon me what Christ had done for us in a way that I have never forgotten.

I was no longer under condemnation. "There is now no condemnation to them which are in Christ Jesus, who walk not after the flesh but after the Spirit."

# 19

## It's Going to Be Okay

### Romans 8:28

I WAS ON the track team in high school. I ran what we called the 440 back then. It was 440 yards or one time around the track. Today it's called the 400, as they measure it in meters. It's still one time around the track or a quarter of a mile. I would run the quarter in the regular 440 race and then again on the mile relay team. The mile relay was one of the last events in the track meet. Each man would run one lap around the track, passing the baton to the next. This was probably my favorite race.

Sometimes, in a close meet, the outcome of the meet could come down to these last races. We would have to win or place in the mile relay to accumulate enough points to win the meet. But sometimes, we would accumulate so many points in the earlier field events, such as pole vault, high jump, shot put, etc., as well as in the earlier races that the meet was already won. We didn't even have to place in this final race because there were not enough points left for the opponents to catch up and win. In these cases, we were running from victory and not to victory. Though we were still running, the meet was already won, just like the victory formation toward the end of a football game. The team is not trying to run a play so they can score and win the game. The game is already won; they are just running out the clock. They are playing from victory.

## WHERE ARE WE GOING TODAY, LORD?

As Christians, we are running from victory and not to victory. The race, the battle, is already won. However, as Paul said in Second Timothy 3:7, we are to run our course faithfully and finish our course.

# 20

## No Separation

### Romans 8:35–39

WHEN LOU ELLEN and I were dating, I picked her and her picnic basket up early one morning for a ride up to the Blue Ridge Parkway in the Blue Ridge Mountains. Her picnic basket was filled with fried chicken, potato salad, deviled eggs, and a lot of other goodies. We were going to find us a waterfall somewhere along the way and enjoy our time together, as well as a good meal.

This was before cell phones and GPS. We would use maps to help us get where we were going if we weren't sure of the way. I gave Lou Ellen the map so she could give me directions while I drove. It would have been hard to drive up a winding road and read the map at the same time. We were having a great time talking nonstop as we traveled along. She would occasionally tell me to take this road or that one. I was looking forward to reaching the Blue Ridge Parkway and finding that perfect spot to enjoy our meal.

After a while, she told me to turn on a little paved road. Something didn't feel right. Then the pavement ran out. We were now driving on a dirt road. She assured me this would take us to the parkway. She said we were almost there, just a little bit farther. We both began to get nervous as the road became a steep climb up the mountain. It was now only one lane, and there was nowhere to turn around. On my left was the side of the mountain covered in trees.

## WHERE ARE WE GOING TODAY, LORD?

On my right was a drop-off going deep into the valley. I was praying I wouldn't meet anyone coming down the mountain, or we were going to have a problem. Though she was nervous and kept reminding me of the drop-off, she also kept telling me we were almost to the parkway. I had my doubts. I really didn't have much choice except to keep driving and praying we would get there or at least find a place to turn around. I certainly didn't want to try to back down that winding road. We finally reached the top. We didn't fall off the side of the mountain. Thank You, Lord. We were now sitting in a small clearing, just big enough to circle around so you could drive forward down the mountain. The parkway? There it was. We could see it with cars going both ways. Lou Ellen said, "There it is." There was only one problem: There was another deep valley between us—so close yet so far away. I took the map from Lou Ellen and looked at it. As she showed me the road she had put us on, I noticed one minor detail. The tiny line representing the road we were on didn't actually touch the big line representing the parkway. As I pointed out that the lines didn't touch, meaning the roads aren't connected, she informed me that they almost touch, and it did get us to the parkway. She had figured it would be close enough; we could find it. We just laughed.

We began the ride down that particular mountain ridge, once again praying we wouldn't meet anyone along the way. We were both getting pretty hungry by now. We found ourselves a little trickle of a waterfall and sat down to eat. It wasn't the waterfall we had anticipated. In fact, much of this adventure had not been what we had planned on. But the food was still good, and the fellowship with each other, surrounded by God's beautiful creation, was fantastic. We saw parts of the Blue Ridge Mountains I had never seen before.

We never made it to the parkway to enjoy one of the most beautiful drives in the country. We could see it. We were close, but we were separated from it by a deep valley that we could not cross in our car.

We had no idea, as I drove and Lou Ellen was sitting by me with the map, that the day was coming when she not only would become an excellent map reader but would be navigating as we drove all over this country, sharing the good news of Jesus.

I went to marine corps boot camp, Parris Island, South Carolina, on December 27, 1971. It was both difficult and rewarding. It helped to prepare me for much of what God had in mind for me.

Toward the end of boot camp, we were allowed to have a visit from our family. Lou Ellen (my future bride), my mom, dad, sister, and brother-in-law came to visit. My dad had served in the navy during WWII and the Korean War. Tom, my brother-in-law, had served in a marine artillery unit in Vietnam.

They arrived the evening before the visit, so my brother-in-law, who had gone through Parris Island, was showing them areas that were open to visitors. They came to the parade deck near the rifle range in hopes of seeing some recruits marching. We were in the barracks at the rifle range when they came.

We were coming out of the mess hall near the parade deck. I was a squad leader, so I took my spot at the head of one of the columns, while the recruits filled in as they came out. They noticed the civilians on the other side of the parade deck. We were not supposed to be speaking, but I whispered down the column that it was my family and that the young lady was my future wife. It was all I could do to stand there and not show excitement. The drill sergeant saw them as well and decided he would entertain them (not knowing they were there to visit one of his recruits). He began marching us around and getting closer and closer to them. We made all kinds of moves getting a little closer each time. Finally, he marched us straight for them. I struggled so hard not to show any emotions on my face. I was praying none of them would call out or wave at me. My dad and Tom knew that would get me in trouble.

He marched us right up to them. Being at the front of one of the four squads, I was close enough to reach my hand forward and touch Lou Ellen when he stopped us. All my family was smiling and laughing but fortunately did not say a word or call me by name.

I was so close yet separated. I didn't sleep much that night, knowing that at some point, the next day I would be called to the visitor's center and would be granted a short visit. But until then, there was a separation.

## WHERE ARE WE GOING TODAY, LORD?

Romans 8 tells us that there is nothing—no mountain or valley or parade deck or drill instructor or anything else—that can separate us from the love of God. What a Savior and constant companion.

# 21

## Respect for the One True God

### Deuteronomy 5:1, 6–10

WHILE MINISTERING IN a tribal village in another country, I met with a young lady. I asked her, "What do you worship?" I didn't ask her who, but what because I knew they were worshipping false gods of wood, stone, and even animals. She named one of the many gods they worshipped. I asked her where it was. She told me it was in her hut. I had seen many of them in their homes and around the area. I said, "Where are you?" She seemed a little puzzled by the question but told me she was standing in front of me. I asked her to tell me what she would do if she needed her god right now. She said she would go back to her hut or find another one of the same image. I asked her to tell me where she got it. She told me her husband brought it home. I asked her how he got it and where it came from. She told me, a man made it and sold it in the market. Her husband bought it and brought it home.

    I went on to ask her what they would do if they needed the god outside. How would it get there? She told me, her husband would bring it outside. I could tell she was getting a little impatient with me. I asked her how it would get back inside for the night. Once again, she told me her husband would move it. She was really getting tired of my questions. But wanting to get the supplies we were giving away, she continued our conversation. She told me they usually didn't move it.

I thanked her for being patient with me. I told her I had one final question for her: "If we bury it, how does it get out of the grave?" The idea of doing such a thing bothered her at first. She told me her husband would dig it out and clean it up.

So far, she had told me that her god was created by man and was dependent on man. I said to her, "It seems your god depends on your husband and can't do anything for itself." She told me she had never thought of it like that.

A crowd had gathered and was listening to our conversation. I said, "Let me tell you about the One true God that is with you wherever you go. He wasn't created by man but created man. He died for you and came out of the grave for you." As we continued that day, this lady and many others became faithful followers of Jesus.

I heard someone say, "If you have a created image, you possess it. But God possesses us. He bought us with a price." Why would we want to follow and worship anyone else?

# 22

## Respect for Life and Language

### Deuteronomy 5:1, 11

IN THE 1970S, while serving on active duty with the US Marines, I was trained in the use of a gas mask. Anyone who served in the military back then probably remembers well their gas mask training. When you hear someone say "gas," you were to immediately hold your breath. You were to make sure you didn't breathe any air through your, nose even though your mouth was shut. Then you would reach for the pouch on your side that contained your mask, pull it out as quickly as you could, and place it over your face. Then you would exhale through your mouth and nose as hard as you could to remove any gas that may have been captured in your mask as you pulled it up to your head. Make sure to mask it tight and breathe naturally. Simple. We'd done it many times in training.

That morning, as we went out, we were told to carry our masks. He wanted us to get used to having something a little bulky on our side. Something was telling me it was a bit more than that. I knew we would be in the woods that day and felt something was up. A little after lunch, we gathered in an outdoor classroom. A cement floor had been poured big enough to hold a platoon of marines. There were several posts holding up a roof. It was actually a nice outdoor classroom. It was better than just sitting on the ground.

## WHERE ARE WE GOING TODAY, LORD?

I don't remember what we were being taught in that particular class, but I remember well what happened. I was sitting in the second row when I heard popping sounds all around me. Immediately, someone shouted, "Gas!" Military-grade tear gas grenades had been dropped by the instructors all around us. Smoke clouds were covering the area. I held my breath and reached for my mask. I could feel my face and neck burning from the gas. It seemed to burn freshly shaven skin. I quickly put the mask on and blew out with all I had. I didn't want to take a breath. What if some of the gas had gotten in my mask, and I didn't get it out? What if the mask didn't work? I had no choice but to try to breathe. It worked. I followed the directions, and it worked. I could easily breathe without any difficulty.

That wasn't the case with everyone. Some of the guys forgot their training. Forgetting their instructions, they panicked. One took off, running away from the area. He couldn't see because of the gas and ran right into a tree. A couple ran into the poles, holding the roof over the classroom. Their noses were running, and their eyes were watering. But for those who followed the instructions, things weren't so bad, even in the midst of the chaos all around us.

God's word is our instructions. It's our training. It tells us how life is designed to be lived. In this passage, His word tells us not to take His name in vain. The way we use His name is an indication of our relationship with Him.

We usually think of our language when we think of this commandment. When I was a little kid, I thought profanity must be really bad because it had its own commandment. We are told not to curse. That's true; we should not use profanity

But the commandment means more than just profanity. The word translated "take" in verse 11, meaning to take on or to carry. That means we should not take on or carry the Lord's name in vain. The word *vain* means empty or insincere.

In other words, we are not to take on the Lord's name and call ourselves a Christian and act like the Lord doesn't matter.

# 23

## Respect for Property

### Deuteronomy 5:1, 19

I REMEMBER, AS a kid, stopping at the old produce stands next to someone's farm or garden. Sometimes no one would be there. A sign would tell what each item cost. There was often a scale to weigh the product. You would take what you wanted to purchase and put the money in a bucket or basket. You would take your change from what was already in the basket.

People would do the same on Halloween. Some people would leave candy on their porches with a sign telling how many pieces of candy to take. This may be amazing to many today, but most would do what the sign said and would not take or steal the whole container of candy, which would mess things up for those who might come after them.

I'm also old enough to remember pulling up to the gas pumps and pumping your gas before you paid for it. After pumping your gas, you would walk inside and pay for your gas. The pumps didn't take cards back then.

Then one day they began changing it to where you had to go in and pay for your gas before you pumped it. This was aggravating because you often didn't know exactly how much gas you might need to pump if you were filling up. Sometimes, if you paid too much, you'd have to go back in a second time to get your change. Or if you didn't pay enough, the pump would stop before the tank was full. This was time-consuming. People began to fuss and complain to the store clerks and the various store owners.

But whose fault was it? The reason that went into effect was because there were too many drive offs, where the people simply drove off without paying. It was a lot easier to get away with it back then when there weren't so many cameras watching the pumps. People seem to forget that the Lord is always watching. I often hear people complaining about cameras being everywhere. These companies would not spend so much money on these security systems if there weren't so many dishonest people stealing from them or committing other crimes.

Many businesses no longer take checks today because they receive too many bad checks. A restaurant owner showed me a drawer full of worthless checks he had received as payment. He said it had gotten so bad he could not afford to stay in business if he kept taking checks for payment.

We have removed the ideals of the Scriptures from our school and TV shows, and people don't seem to have the character not to take what is not theirs.

Our second pastorate had a parsonage about a half mile from the church. It had a double garage separate from the house. There were no doors on the front of the garage, where you drove your vehicles in. At the back of the garage was a storage room with locking doors, where we had a chest freezer.

We had a very fruitful garden that summer and had a lot of vegetables in the freezer. We also had many jars of green beans, tomatoes, etc., in the house, which we had canned. The freezer also contained a fully processed hog, which someone had given us right before we left to come to this church. There was a side of beef as well. It had been difficult to spend the money for the side of beef, but we knew we would come out ahead in the long run. To go along with all of that, we had two frozen turkeys we had been given. I couldn't think of a time in our lives when we had such a stockpile of food. The Lord had always provided as we needed. We were certainly ready for winter.

As we came in one Wednesday night, after services, and were pulling into the garage, I noticed the door to the room with the freezer was open. When I looked into the freezer, everything was gone. Well, almost everything. The thief had good taste as he left both the beef and pork liver. That's the one thing I don't eat. My wife likes it, but I will pass. We also found a turkey he dropped in the yard as he was leaving. We found out that the freezer at the elementary school down the road had been robbed as well. Apparently, the thieves knew that the school freezer had been filled that day and that we had received the side of beef the day before. They had good information on when to rob us. They knew the preacher and his family would be at church on a Wednesday night.

In the 1960s, while I was in high school, I was working at a Bi-Lo grocery store as a stocker. It was one of their original stores. One afternoon, the lights went out. It was still light outside, but the store was dark inside, except for the checkout area in the front of the store, where the giant windows across the front let some light in.

The light through the windows made it possible for those up front to see and check the customers out. Each stocker went and stood next to one of the cashiers to turn the crank on the side of the cash register each time the cashier punched in a number. There were no computerized cash registers or bar codes at that time. When the power went out, the registers would work like the old times, adding machines when cranked. So I stood there, cranking the register each time she punched in the price of the item. She was using one hand to punch in the number and the other hand to slide the item into the bagging area. We were handling the situation well and our customers were being taken care of. They had to quit shopping because they couldn't see in the aisles, but they did get to check out what they already had.

The lights were only out for about thirty minutes. When they came back on, we were surprised at what had taken place in the dark. The store changed their procedures after that. On the aisle that contained aspirin, stomach medicine, etc., there were empty boxes on the floor—a lot of empty boxes. Some of the customers (thieves) had taken the items out of the boxes and placed them in their purses. The store was not checking purses as they were leaving. The store took a big loss on that day. After that day, we were told to go to our aisles with a flashlight to help guide the customers when the lights went out. This was to protect the store, as well as help the customers.

Stealing is a universal problem. While on one of my earlier mission trips to India, we had gone to the city to pick up some things. I accompanied one of our nurses to the bank so she could exchange a traveler's check for Indian currency. She handed the clerk her passport as identification and reached into her bag to retrieve her traveler's check. As she pulled it out, she had the strangest look on her face. I noticed that the check in her hand had been folded several times and was rather dirty. As she unfolded it, her expression changed even more. She looked at me, as if she didn't know what to say. She began to apologize to me and said she had no idea how she had gotten this particular check. It was evident she was afraid of what my reaction was going to be. She handed me the check. I was shocked myself when I saw it. It had my name on it. She had one of my checks. I assured her that I knew she had not been in my stuff and had not taken one of my checks.

Apparently, someone had stolen one of my checks, thinking it was American currency. They had folded it and placed it in their waistline or pocket as they often did. This is why it was so dirty. When they found out it was a traveler's check and they could not use it without proper identification that matched the check, they tried to return it. However, for whatever reason, they placed it in her purse instead of returning it to me.

Once again, I assured the nurse that I knew she had not stolen one of my checks and that everything was okay. We were good friends, and I knew she wouldn't do that. She then pulled out her check and exchanged it for the Indian currency. We did have fun kidding each other about the incident in the days that followed.

Someone said it well when they said, "If I have $10. and you steal it, I have lost $10. But you have lost much more. You have lost your self-respect and know yourself to be a thief."

# 24

## Respect for the Lord's Day

### Deuteronomy 5:12–15

I REMEMBER ONE day, as a kid, I tried to make brownies. They did not turn out like Mom's. There was nothing wrong with the recipe. There was nothing wrong with the ingredients. The problem was that I didn't follow the recipe or the instructions. I was little and could not read that well back then. I made a simple mistake. I switched the salt and sugar. I put a dash of sugar and a cup of salt. It's amazing what a difference switching two ingredients can make. You don't want to try making brownies that way. They didn't taste like Mom's.

The world is in a mess because it is not following the directions from the One Who created it. God's word is our recipe, our instructions for life.

God knew we would need a special time for rest and worship. He gave us this commandment for our benefit.

It is a well-known fact that our bodies must have periods of rest. A preacher once told me he'd rather burn out than rust out. I understood what he was saying. I've never been lazy, but as I've gotten older, I've come to realize that I will burn out a lot sooner and should therefore do a lot less for the kingdom if I don't have periods of rest as we were designed to have by our Creator.

But this passage is not just talking about physical rest. It's talking about spiritual rest and worship as well.

The Lord knew how easy it would be for us to get so caught up in our daily activities that we forget Him. He set this time aside for us to worship and spend time in His presence in His house. This is not only one of the most important parts of our week but the most rewarding as well. Hebrews 10:25 tells us that taking part in the local church is not optional for the child of God. How can we say we love the Lord and not be faithful to His church? It's Christian worship and fellowship that helps us to grow in the faith.

How many times do you find yourself having arguments before coming to church? How many times do you get upset because you are running late? If you are a Sunday school teacher, how many times do you find yourself rushing around on Sunday morning, trying to prepare a lesson you should have worked on all week?

We ought to get up each Sunday morning with excitement and expectation because we are going to God's house. It's better than a ball game, and I love ball games.

# 25

## Does It Fit?

### First Samuel 17:38-39

THE SUMMER BETWEEN my freshman and sophomore years of college, I was working in construction. We had a flagman who was all excited about taking karate. He sounded like he had been taking for years. During our lunch break, he pulled out a pair of nunchaku. As it turned out, he'd only had three lessons but had already purchased a pair of nunchaku. He began to demonstrate how to use them. Almost immediately, as he was waving them around his back to catch them over his shoulder, he hit himself in the back of the head. The sudden blow to the back of his head dropped him to his knees. He was not seriously hurt but could have been. I will never forget the startled look on his face as the wooden stick hit him.

I couldn't help but think of young David, in 1 Samuel 17:38-39, when he was trying on Saul's armor so he could go out and fight Goliath. Saul was trying to help when he offered his armor to David. Imagine going to battle wearing the king's personal armor. But there was a problem: David was still a kid, probably a teenager. It didn't fit. It was too heavy. And in his days as a shepherd, he'd never used any armor. I'm sure the armor was very nice, but David didn't know how to use it. You can't go to battle with someone else's armor. God had already prepared David with what he needed: a sling.

## WHERE ARE WE GOING TODAY, LORD?

There was a pastor I had grown very fond of. I was serving as a minister of music and youth at a church in the same town he was serving as pastor. Though we were serving in different churches, we had gotten to know each other through various meetings. He had taken an interest in mentoring a younger minister. My wife and I would often fellowship with his wife and family.

One day, he called me and told me they had an opening for a full-time minister of discipleship. I really wanted to work with him. I was all excited as I told my wife about the opportunity. We were still newlyweds. But the more I prayed about it, the more I was convinced that was not the Lord's will for us. As important as the discipleship position was, it was not what I had been called to do and was not where my gifts and abilities were. I would be going to battle without the proper armor. As much as I wanted to work with and learn from this pastor, I had to turn down the opportunity. It was what I wanted and not what I was called to do. God was not yet through with me where I was.

A short time later, I was contacted again and told that the minister of music at his church had resigned. I ended up going there and serving with this pastor but in the position that I had been called to serve. I learned a lot from this pastor, not realizing it was preparing me for when the Lord called me to become a pastor. We serve best when we serve where the Lord leads, using that which He has given us.

# 26

## Respect for the Truth

### Deuteronomy 5:1, 20

A YOUNG LADY, whom we know, came to work one day. As she was turning her computer on and getting ready for a day of work, she was approached and told she was being suspended from work for using drugs. They took her to a nearby facility, where she could have a blood test done to see what drugs she had been using. She was suspended for three days while they were waiting for the result to come back. When the blood test came back, it showed there were no drugs in her system. She was completely innocent. She had missed three days of work and had been embarrassed in front of her peers as they had told her she had to have this drug test and was not to come back to work until the results were in. It all happened because another employee was jealous of her and started the rumor that she was using drugs.

Lives have been ruined because of false rumors and gossip someone has spread. Many speak out about other people's sins but pay no attention to their own sin of lying.

I had a lady in one church who was very good at spreading gossip. She was the queen of gossip. She would even start false rumors about church members.

Her husband was serving as a deacon (the Bible speaks about deacon's wives). I noticed that no matter what the deacons discussed in their meetings, the next day, she was talking about it.

One deacons' meeting, I told them we had a problem with a lady in the church gossiping and that it was harming the church, and we needed to deal with it. They agreed. I told the chairman he would need to come with me. I also said I wanted one other deacon to come with us as well. Her husband, not realizing I was talking about his wife, volunteered (how he didn't know, I don't understand). I told them, if I heard one more word about this lady and her gossip, I would call them, and we would make the visit to talk with her. And if she continued to spread her gossip, we would take it before the church.

I could picture him telling his wife what was said in the meeting, especially when he told her he would be one of the ones going to talk to this church gossip. She suddenly became very quiet, and we didn't have to make the visit.

In one small church, the pastor used to council people in the sanctuary as he didn't have an office at the church suitable for doing so. He would sit in one of the chairs used for Communion, next to the Communion table. The person being counseled would sit on the front pew. However, the members began to wonder if the pastor was sharing with others what was being said in those sessions. It seemed what they were talking about was getting out to others. The pastor was getting into trouble over this. He knew he had not shared anything, not even to his wife. In fact, his wife, understanding the counseling relationship, never asked him about what was said or who he had been talking to.

Behind the sanctuary was a narrow hallway, which had a door leading to the baptistry. The door had a doorknob like you would have on your bedroom or bathroom door. It had a simple push-button lock on it. It seems when they needed a door for the baptistry, someone said they had a door they had removed from their bedroom. They gave it to the church. The locking doorknob was left on the door. The button used to lock the door was left on the hallway side of the door. They always said they needed to change it before the kids lock someone in the baptistry.

One afternoon, the pastor was meeting someone in the sanctuary. He said he didn't know what caused him to do it, but as he was walking down the hallway behind the sanctuary, he reached out and pushed that button as he walked by locking the door.

As he finished counseling and was leaving, he heard a voice. As he turned around, he saw a lady's head sticking up from inside the baptistry. She asked if he would let her out. She said she had gone in there to see if it needed swept out or cleaned in any way before the next baptism. It turned out that if she saw certain people's car parked in the parking lot, she would often sneak into the baptistry and sit on the steps leading into the tank so she could hear what was being said. She would then spread the gossip. On this occasion, she had heard the person mention that she was going to speak with the pastor so she had walked to the church first.

The preacher had been falsely accused of sharing everything people had told him in confidence. He had been accused of spreading gossip. This could have destroyed his ministry when he was completely innocent.

I know of a man who took his family to the beach. They were having a great time and were wishing they had a couple more days of vacation. The father was supposed to return to work on Monday. However, he called his boss and told him that he would not be able to return to work on time because he had gotten sick. He said a doctor had told him he had sun poisoning and was going to have to stay in his motel room for a couple of days before coming home. He said he hoped to be able to return to work on Wednesday. After making the call to his boss, he returned to the beach and enjoyed the sun and the ocean. What kind of example was he setting for his family?

We are so quick to sacrifice the truth. God did not create relationships to be built on lies. It doesn't work that way. Proverbs 6:16–19 lists seven things God hates. Three of them—lying tongue, false witness who speaks lies, and one who sows discord among brethren—have to do with the tongue and bearing false witness.

# 27

## Just Say Yes

### Mark 10:35–45

WHEN MY CHILDREN were little, they would sometimes come up to me and say, "Daddy, just say yes."

I'd ask, "Yes to what?"

They would say, "Just say yes."

They usually knew what my answer might be if I knew what they were wanting. I would tell them, "If I don't know what it is, the answer is no."

In Mark 10:35, James and John were asking Jesus to say yes to whatever they desired. They wanted a blank check. What is important is what they didn't say. They didn't say what they wanted. I wonder why?

If Jesus had given them what they asked for (Mark 10:37: one to sit on His right and the other to sit on His left when He entered into his kingdom), what do you think would have happened? In their culture, the right side of the king was the most prominent, while the left was next. They probably would have gotten into an argument over which would sit on his right.

Can you hear them? "I'm older." "But I'm smarter." "I'm stronger." "I met Jesus first." "I'm better looking." They could have lost fellowship with each other.

I knew one man who was badly henpecked at home and was taken advantage of and picked on at work. So he went after authority in church. There he had some say, so he made it difficult for everyone. Of course, I think his wife was telling him what to say and do when he got to the church. Power and authority are not what it is all about. We have too many who only want position, power, authority, and attention.

The disciples had not yet learned that it is faithful service and not selfish desires that is important. They had the wrong motive.

After about eight years in Kentucky as a seminary student and then pastor of a church, we moved back to South Carolina. The Lord had called us to a church.

Lou Ellen went to work with a temp company that sent her to a large law firm. She knew the job would only be available until the previous person returned from having knee surgery.

She did whatever was asked of her, no matter how menial or important it was. Shortly before the girl was to return, Lou Ellen was called into a meeting, where fourteen of the law partners were sitting. She took them what they needed and left the large conference room. She had no idea she was one of the topics on their agenda. After the meeting was finished, she found out they were not about to let her get away. They knew it was only right for the other girl to return but had noticed how the mood of the office had changed and how efficient she had been in whatever, big or small, she had been asked to do.

They created a new position, with full benefits for her. She would be available to fill in for any one of the attorneys who needed her.

She began as a servant. She was happy to have that position. So the Lord blessed her with a much greater one.

A couple in Arkansas owned a large logging company, as well as other businesses. They had done very well for themselves and had a nice place to live with nice vehicles.

They were members of a small church. When we were leading a revival in that church, we parked our RV in their driveway and stayed in their pool house. It was very nice. It had a kitchen, bathroom, and a den-bedroom combination. I enjoyed the pool after my early morning run.

What was amazing about them was how much they gave to others and the volunteer work they did. While he would be at work, she would be volunteering at the school or some other project, often getting dirty and working hard in the task. They were humble and compassionate. Even though they had plenty and could have sat back and had everyone serving them, they still saw themselves as servants for Christ.

The world needs people whose desire is to serve.

I've met many who wanted the attention of being a missionary or evangelist but didn't want to serve or actually do the work.

# 28

## The Way We Were Designed to Live

### Deuteronomy 5:1

MY FIRST CAR was a 1958 Volkswagen Bug. I loved that car. It had a large sunroof. To open it, you had to reach up and turn a lever and slide a thick canvas top back to let the sun and wind come in. Of course, there was no air-conditioning. In fact, it didn't even have a gas gauge. I'm not sure what year they started putting gas gauges in their cars. The car had a ten-gallon tank. I got thirty miles to the gallon, so that was sufficient. You had to drive the car until it started skipping from a lack of gas. Then you had to quickly reach down and turn a lever on the floor to release a gallon of gas from the reserve tank. It would dump into the regular tank and give you another thirty miles to go and find some gas. The important thing to remember was to always flip the lever back after you filled your tank. If you didn't, your heart would sink when you bent over to release your reserve and found out that it had already poured into the regular tank. I only did that once.

Another unique thing about the car was that it didn't have a radiator. You never had to put water or antifreeze in it. It was air-cooled. Because there was no water, there was no heater. You turned a knob, which was supposed to let heat coming off the engine warm up the car. It didn't work very well, so I always had to wear a coat when driving in the winter. But it was designed to work without putting water into it. If I tried to operate the truck I drive now without water and antifreeze, I would soon be in trouble. I would destroy the engine. I could throw the instruction manual away and operate it like I did my Volkswagen but only for a very short time because it was not designed to operate without putting water in it. That's why the owner's manual tells you to keep a check on the water level. The Volkswagen, on the other hand, was designed to work without water, so it was fine without it.

Human flesh is not designed to be placed against extreme heat. To break that boundary, to place your flesh against extreme heat, means you must bear the results. We should know better.

A very young girl, whose name I will not mention, told me about sitting on the kitchen counter next to the stove. Her mom had been cooking. As she was talking with her mom, she slid over onto the eye of the stove. Even though her mom had turned the stove off and the burner was no longer red, it was still hot and burned the little girl. She didn't mean to put her flesh against the eye of the stove, but she did. As a result, she paid the consequences of doing so. She burned herself and found it a little uncomfortable sitting for a while.

I was at marine corps boot camp at Parris Island. At the time I was there, they had steam pipes everywhere. They used steam for heating, etc. One day, I was told to remove some dust that had settled on a steam pipe. I reacted immediately and quickly removed the dust. There was one problem: I didn't get a rag to wipe it off. I simply took my right hand and wiped it across the pipe (you have to understand the situation at boot camp). How long do you think it took me to realize this was not a good idea? I heard a sizzle and felt pain in my hand. I said nothing and didn't let out a yell, even though it was hurting. Why did I have to use my right hand? That night, during inspection, the DIs (drill instructors) were walking by each one of us and checking to make sure we were all right from the day's activities. When they checked my hands, they saw the blisters. I was sent to sick bay, where they were bandaged and treated. This caused me some problems for the next several days.

Going against the way life was designed to be lived results in consequences that can be painful or destructive.

When we go against God's instructions for our lives, His word in the Scriptures, we pay the consequences. God knows how we were designed to live.

# 29

## You Talking to Me?

### Mark 10:42–45

THE SOUTHERN BAPTIST Convention used to draw thousands of messengers from all over the country, as well as from other countries. It was held in a different city each year. At one time, there were only a few cities that could handle the number of hotel rooms and convention space that was required to host the convention. It brought a lot of money to the host city.

Lou Ellen and I always enjoyed going to the Afterglow and other various gatherings after the day's sessions had ended. The Afterglow was often very late at night. On one particular night, we walked into a big banquet room, with chairs lining the walls. The middle of the room was open for people to mingle. I noticed a group gathered together that included past convention presidents and other well-known leaders in the convention. They had grouped together. Others began to congregate around them as they wanted to meet and speak to these leaders of the SBC (Southern Baptist Convention).

Adrian Rogers entered the room. Everyone there knew who he was. He had served as president of the convention and pastored one of the larger churches in the country. He was also well-known for his radio broadcasts. As he entered the room, he did not head toward all the other dignitaries in the room. When someone from the group called for him to join them, he said he'd be there in a minute. You see, Dr. Rogers's eyes had caught a young preacher sitting by himself in one of the chairs against the wall. Dr. Rogers walked straight to the man everyone else had failed to notice. It shocked the young man as he saw Adrian standing in front of him. Dr. Rogers stuck out his hand to the young man and said, "Hello, I'm Adrian Rogers. May I sit next to you for a bit?"

The startled young man started to stand up as he reached forward to shake hands. Adrian gently placed his hand on his shoulder and told him not to get up. The young man told him he knew who he was. Adrian said, "Well, tell me who you are and about your ministry." They talked a little while before Adrian told him he had to get up and speak to the others but hoped they would get to talk again sometime.

What an influence he must have had on that young man. Dr. Rogers continued to understand that it is about service and not position. He understood his position and status was to open doors for service and not to be served.

As you study the Scriptures, you notice Jesus always called and reached out to everyone, especially those society would ignore. The world looks to the prominent, but Jesus looks to all of us, regardless of our position or status.

Several years ago, we were attending a banquet with evangelists from around the country. Lou Ellen and I sat down at a table next to the stage. We were the first ones to sit at that table. Each table held about eight people. A young man in jeans was on the stage, checking a mic and placing a guitar on the guitar stand. At first, I thought he might be a stagehand. But then I noticed everyone was wanting to speak to him and shake his hand. I began to wonder who he was. Lou Ellen recognized him but hadn't told me who he was. She thought I knew.

Then the fellow sat down at our table. That way, he'd be close to the stage when it was time for him to sing. It was amazing how quickly our table filled after he sat down. We were a ways into the meal before I realized who he was. From the conversations, I knew he was well-known (at least they all knew who he was). Someone asked him about entertaining the troops overseas and other things he had done. Following the meal, he went to the stage, took his guitar, sang, and ministered to us. I recognized his voice and music when he began to sing.

After he finished ministering to us, he came over and began talking to Lou Ellen and me. We had gotten up from the table. The conversation became more personal as he poured his heart out to us. We spent some more time with him over the next couple of days. Many there, probably most there, would say they would love to have his schedule and to be in his shoes. He was traveling all over and was achieving much acclaim. He was famous and well-known. The funny thing is, many people wanted to speak to us just because we seemed to know him. They had no idea he was hurting and going through some difficult times, just like everyone else. Many would not have been willing to change their position for his, had they known.

Quit wishing you were someone else or had what someone else has. Just be what God called you to be and serve Him how, when, and where He calls you to serve Him, whether you become part of the rich and famous or the poor and unknown. It's about servanthood.

# 30

## Destroyed from Within

### Galatians 5:19–21

HISTORY SHOWS US that sometimes the greatest threat to a nation is not what attacks it from without but what attacks it from within.

I was at Lake Greenwood at my in-laws' lake house. I got up for an early morning run. I really enjoyed running there. When I finished my run, I sat in a chair on the porch. It was one of those old metal slider rockers. Some of you may remember them. It was very comfortable. Lou Ellen's dad had recently painted it, and it really looked good. I was enjoying sitting there while I was waiting for my oxygen to catch up with me. I was thinking about our upcoming schedule and how God had blessed us with a great place to catch a little rest before we were back on the road.

Lou Ellen and her parents had gotten up and were inside, talking and looking out the window.

Everything was fine until I heard a noise, and the next thing I knew, the chair flipped back. I was sitting on my back with my feet and legs sticking up in front of the window. The chair had broken and fallen back.

I was expecting my loved ones inside to see my situation and come running out or maybe say something like, "Oh, no, I hope he's all right." What I heard was a lot of laughing. Lou Ellen did come out to check on me. I wasn't hurt but was a little embarrassed.

Even though the chair looked great from the outside, fresh paint and all, water had been collecting in the metal tubing of the frame. Over time, it had been rusting through. I just happened to be the one sitting there when the rust finished doing what rust does: It ate its way through.

The chair was corrupted and destroyed from within. While my family got a good laugh, it is not funny when it is happening to our nation. We'd be careful.

# 31

## The Old Faithful Preacher

### Acts 21:16; Matthew 25:23

MNASON IS REFERRED to in the King James Version as an old disciple. In the New King James Version, he referred to as an early disciple. It indicates that he had been a Christian for a long time and was probably an older man. He is not mentioned anywhere else in the Scriptures. There were no great messages he preached or miracles he took part in. We are simply told he was a faithful Christian, who was devoted to the Lord and expressed his love for the Lord by opening his home up to Paul and others. He reminds me of so many others who remain faithful to the Lord without any earthly recognition.

We were having a missions and evangelism conference in a large church.

Preaching and music evangelists were leading in the services being held each morning and evening. Classes on different aspects of ministry were being led by the evangelists each afternoon.

We asked local pastors to lead the prayer time and had different churches bring their choirs. As the evening service was about to begin, an elderly pastor, who was to give the opening prayer, became emotional as he was about to walk up to the pulpit. When asked if he was all right, he said he was fine, just excited and grateful. He said he had pastored small churches for forty years and had never been asked to take part in a large meeting. He had never stood in the pulpit of such a large church. He said he was both nervous and grateful that the Lord had allowed him to do so that night.

I don't know why he had never been asked to take part in a service such as this before. But what I do know is that the Lord has a special reward for this faithful preacher when his work is done. I believe men and women such as this may very well have greater rewards in heaven than some of those who are in large churches. He was faithful to what the Lord had called him to do and remained humble.

# 32

## No Idea How Long We Have

Matthew 25:14–18

GROWING UP, AS a kid, we were able to roam the neighborhood a lot more than kids today. During the summer, when school was out, Mom and Dad would go to work, and we would ride our bikes to our friend's house, play in the nearby woods, or play ball.

Sometimes, before going to work, Mom or Dad would give me chores to do before they returned. Now I knew exactly when my mom would be coming home. I knew what time she got off and how long it would take her to get home. It never varied much. So when she gave me a job to do, I knew how long I could wait before I had to take care of it. However, it was different with my dad, much different. He worked all over town, and I never knew when he might drop by to check on what he had asked me to do. If it was cutting the grass, I knew I'd better get started early because I didn't want him to drive by and not see me working. I never knew how long I had before he might come by.

During the 1970s, a pastor (he had never married) that I knew didn't show up at church one Sunday morning. During the Sunday school hour, many were joking that he had probably overslept. They tried to call him on the phone, but he didn't answer. When it was time for the worship service to start, a couple of deacons walked next door to check on him. He didn't come to the door. His car was in the driveway. They got the custodian to bring a key from the church office so they could go in. They called his name as they entered—still no answer. When they went into his bedroom, he was still lying in bed. He had died sometime during the night from a heart attack. He was not overweight, nor had he had any known health problems.

I'm sure he had all kinds of plans for that day. What was he going to preach? Where was he going to eat lunch? Who was he going to see? And what meetings might he be having? But he didn't know his time was up and that he wouldn't be carrying out any of those plans.

We need to take our responsibility seriously and apply ourselves to what God has called us to do. When the Lord returns or my time here is up, I want to be found faithfully doing that which He has called me to do.

The man in Matthew 25 was called wicked not for what he had done but for what he had not done. He had done nothing.

You may not curse, drink, smoke, or go with those who do. That's just great. I'm happy for you. But what are you doing for Christ with the opportunities and resources He has given you? He is coming back, and we only have so much time.

# 33

## Respect for Parents—Turnabout

### Deuteronomy 5:16

THE FIRST THING established after creation was the home, the family. The family was God's idea and not man's. A lot of the problems we are having as a nation is because we have abandoned God's plan for the family. We are not living the way we were designed to live by the Creator.

My wife's dad had a major stroke. One day, I was watching her as she fixed her dad something to eat. After preparing his meal, she pushed him in his wheelchair to the table. She then helped to feed him as he had no use of his right arm. I thought of how there was a day when she was a baby, and he would roll her around in a stroller before she could walk. I thought of how he probably fed her before she was able to feed herself—turnabout.

Children are to help care for their parents as they get older. To dishonor our parents and fail to care for them is to dishonor God and His word.

# 34

## Decision Time

First Kings 18:17–22

IN HONG KONG, I saw a row of Buddhas. I was told you would pray to one for health, another for wealth, another for happiness, another for a good crop, and another one if you wanted to get pregnant. I guess they were like our doctors-specialists.

I've seen people in other places worship cows, snakes, and gods made of wood and stone—oh, the sorrow of it. Bowing down before helpless gods while the great living God of heaven and earth is always ready to help those who choose to come to call on Him and follow Him.

In 1 Kings 18:17, we see once again that the Scriptures are still up-to-date as people haven't changed through the years. Ahab blamed Elijah for the drought rather than his own idolatry. That is so typical. We always blame someone else. "The fight started when he hit me back." We're walking on a flat sidewalk with nothing in our way, and we trip over our own feet. We immediately look down and point as if something is there that made us trip. We don't want to admit we tripped on our own feet.

While our daughter was still in middle school, a young man died in a car accident. She said many were asking why God would take him when he was so young and keep so many others. I asked, "What do you think?" I went over the sequence leading up to the accident. The Scriptures tell us that we should obey the laws of the land unless they are in violation of the Scriptures themselves. We are also told that our bodies are the temple of the Holy Spirit, so we should take of it. This young man, when he got off work, began drinking a six-pack of beer. (Someone broke the law in either giving it to him or selling it to him). He was also smoking wacky weed (marijuana). He was breaking the law as well as disregarding his body. Then he began driving home. He showed a disregard for the speed limit, again breaking the law and risking not only his health but others as well. We are clearly told to care for others. Then when he came to a sharp turn close to his house, he paid no attention to the drop in the speed limit (which he was already breaking) nor the sign warning him about the turn. Being under the influence of alcohol and marijuana, as well as speeding, he was unable to make the turn. He ran off the road, hitting a tree, resulting in his death. It was tragic. It hurts to see things like this happening. His family and friends are suffering because of his actions. In this case, it was his choice to disregard God's word that had been given for our benefit and not to restrict us. It wasn't God. Don't blame God; He warned us.

> And Elijah came to all the people, and said, How long will you falter between two opinions? If the Lord is God, follow Him; but if baal, follow him. But the people answered him not a word. (1 Kings 18:21)

> No man can serve two masters; for either he will hate the one and love the other, or else he will be loyal to the one and despise the other. You cannot serve God and mammon. (Matthew 6:24)

What if I came in one night and told my wife that I love her and married her because she is number one in my life, but I had run into one of my old girlfriends and was going to give her every Tuesday night? "You're still number one. I'm giving you six nights a week."

## WHERE ARE WE GOING TODAY, LORD?

Then I came in a few weeks later and told my wife that I ran into another girl I use to date and that I was going to give her every Thursday night. "But you are still number one. I'm giving you five nights a week. You are the one I married."

How do you think that would work out?—not only would he bad for my health and well-being, but our relationship would be destroyed.

# 35

## Thou Art the Man

### Second Samuel 12:1–15

I KNEW A man who wanted to get a group of men together to go and beat up a man who would get drunk and beat his wife. He wanted to teach him a lesson. He said he knew I probably wouldn't go, being I was a preacher. (I wouldn't take part even if I wasn't a preacher.) I surprised him by suggesting that we all meet at his house before going to see the man he wanted to beat up. I told him, if that was the way he wanted to handle situations like this, we should beat him up first because I knew he had hit his wife before. After getting over the shock that the preacher knew what he'd done, we had a long talk about what was going on in his life and how he needed to get his sins taken care of rather than going and trying to deal with the other man.

We are too quick to pronounce judgment on others when we are just as guilty. We may not have done the same sins, but we are just as guilty.

We must remember that the purpose of Nathan revealing David's sin was not to ridicule or condemn him but rather to help him restore his relationship with the Lord. Should we ever confront someone about their sin, we should make sure we do it with love and not with malice.

# 36

## Change that Matters

Second Peter 3:18; John 1:40–42, Philippians 3:13

THE VICE PRESIDENT of the local bank was a member of a church I was serving as pastor. We were talking one day, and he told me he didn't like consolidation loans. He said they can be a good tool to help some people, but for most who come in wanting them, they only make their situation worse over time. He said they get into trouble when they have too many different bills each month and don't have enough funds to pay them. They want to get a loan to pay them all off. Then they have to pay on the loan each month. It will be a little high, but they can manage that and still have money left over each month to take care of living expenses. He said, on paper and in theory, it looks like a good idea. For some people, it works well for them. But for many, it becomes a disaster. He said, many of them fail to change their spending habits. The same spending habits that got them in trouble the first time get them into even worse trouble after they get the loan. They see something they want. They know they don't have the money to buy it, but because of the consolidation loan, they now have a few extra dollars on hand, so they purchase it on credit. Then the car breaks down, or something else happens, and they don't have the money to take care of it. They charge that as well.

Now they have even more bills than their salary, plus the large loan they took out to get them out of trouble in the first place.

The first church we served as pastor was in Kentucky. We had a young man in the church some people referred to as Brother Jim's hippie (they called their pastor Brother). His hair hung below his shoulders. He had that hippie look. We got along fine, and our kids loved him. He would often do work for us. He had a substance abuse problem.

One evening, I received a call from a bar a few miles from the church. They told me I needed to come and get him before he got into trouble. He was pretty drunk. I took him home. I often hear about him getting picked up by the local police for public intoxication. He had been to rehab several times, but he continued to drink and take drugs. He had so many possibilities but would not stay clean.

The Lord led us to a church in South Carolina. Early one morning, just before the sun came up, I went out and got into my van to go to the hospital to pray with someone before they had surgery. As I placed my hand across the back of the seat to look behind me as I was backing out of the driveway, a figure popped up from the back and said, "Good morning!" I nearly went through the top of the van. I was not expecting to see a face behind me. It turned out to be Brother Jim's hippie from Kentucky. What was he doing here? After getting over the shock of him being in my van, he explained everything.

He said he had hitchhiked his way from Kentucky. He wanted to get a fresh start in a new environment away from those that had been influencing him. He said he wanted to get a job and his own place to stay. I told him we would help. He stayed with us for a couple of weeks while I helped him get a job and a place to stay. There was a man near us who had an apartment above his garage he wanted to rent. After much discussion, I got him to rent it for half his regular price to help this young man get started. We got him a job working in a furniture store. He would deliver, put together, and help set up furniture. This would be easy work for him.

## WHERE ARE WE GOING TODAY, LORD?

Things went well for several weeks. He was making enough money to pay rent and buy food. It looked like it was going to work out well for him. But then he went back to his old habits. He thought he would just stop in and get a drink one night. One drink won't hurt. He didn't stop with one. Another night, he thought he'd smoke some marijuana. After all, he'd worked hard that day. He could handle it. It wasn't long that he lost his job and apartment. He chose to go back to his old habits, which had gotten him into trouble in the first place. He went back to Kentucky.

Here was a man who could have done so well in life and could have done so much for the Lord. When given the opportunity to have a new start, a change that matters, he threw it all away. When he was in his forties, due to bad health, he was placed in a nursing home. He could hardly walk. He died a young man.

# 37

## One Job to Do

### John 1:6–8, 15–34

WHEN LOU ELLEN and I got married, we received an unusual wedding gift, but we sure did enjoy it. It was a bird dog. That's right, a genuine, first-class bird dog. Is that a great wedding gift or not?

We were serving in a church as minister of music and youth. A man in the church was well-known for the bird dogs he raised. When he had a new litter of puppies at about the same time we were getting married, he told us we could have our pick. When we returned from our honeymoon, we went to his house and picked him out.

Lou Ellen suggested we name him Bullet, after the dog on the Roy Rogers TV show from the fifties. The dog from the show was also referred to as the wonder dog. The name fit because he was fast and supersmart.

The only problem was, we had this beautiful dog, and I knew nothing about training bird dogs. We certainly didn't have the money to pay a professional trainer.

Problem solved. Lou Ellen was working at Park Seed Company in Greenwood, South Carolina, as the secretary to the man you wrote to or called when you had questions on various plants. There was a man who came in each spring to help prepare the grounds for the flower festival they held each year. It was beautiful, and people came from all around to view the grounds. He and Lou Ellen became friends. It turned out, he trained bird dogs. His house was full of trophy dogs he had trained and had received at field trials. He even went to Canada sometimes to train dogs there.

When Lou Ellen told him we had received a bird dog as a wedding present, he said he would train it for free. We could afford that price. We were to leave Bullet with him for a few weeks and bring a couple of fifty-pound bags of dog food to his house.

When we picked him up, he drove us to a field nearby and let Bullet work. It was beautiful to watch. He said we would never lose Bullet because Bullet kept checking back with us. His nose would get the scent. He would quietly work his way up to where the birds were sitting in the tall grass or bush. Then he would lift his front paw, lift his tail, and point his head toward the birds. He wouldn't move until we were ready. Bullet really enjoyed hunting.

Bullet became a member of our family. He was our only child until our daughter was born. But when we went hunting, he had one job: He would point. But he would not point at just anything he saw. His job was to point to the quail. He was good at it.

In John 1, we read about a man named John. He was to be the forerunner of Christ. He had one job, and that was to point people to Christ. He was to prepare the way for the coming of the Messiah, and he was good at it.

John knew that he was not called to become the center of attention, but rather he was called to point to and bring attention to another.

John said in John 3:28 that he had been sent. As we read the Scriptures, we read of others being sent by God. We need to remember that we too have been sent (the Great Commission). It's time we start doing what we have been called to do as Christians, pointing people to Christ.

# 38

## Never Heard of Him

### Luke 1:26–35

ONCE AGAIN, WE find God choosing the insignificant to become the significant.

However, many who follow Jesus may never become well-known or famous. We all know the name Bill Graham. But most would not recognize the name of a man I served under when I was an associate minister. He served faithfully for many years. He never pastored a large church, but he influenced many. He certainly had a big influence on my life and what I am doing today.

Years ago, while I was serving as minister of music and youth, Lou Ellen and I went to all of the local high school games. We had the privilege of watching them win the state championship game.

One of the keys to their success was their kicking game. They had a field goal kicker that practically never missed, even long-range.

For several years, people always praised their kickers. The secret behind their kicking success was not just the kicker himself but their kicking coach. He was a great coach. You never saw him running onto the field during the game or making a kick himself, but he was making a difference as he taught these young kickers the fundamentals of the kicking game.

Everyone knew who the kickers were, but few knew the man behind them who was making such a difference.

God may call on you to be the one on the field that everyone sees. He may call you to be the one quietly making a difference behind the scenes. It may be a combination of the two. But whichever way He chooses to use you, be ready and faithful to that which He has called you to do.

We don't know the names of the ones who lowered Paul over the wall in a basket when others were trying to kill him, but what a difference they made. Paul was able to continue in the ministry because they were faithful to what they had been called to do.

# 39

## Excuse Making

### Luke 10:25–37

IN THIS PASSAGE, we read about the Good Samaritan, who stopped and helped a man in need. But before the good Samaritan came along, there were a couple of guys who came by and didn't do so well. They remind me of some folks I've met in a lot of our churches.

We finished a revival meeting close to where our family lived, so we took a few days to stay with them before we went back on the road. We unhooked the fifth-wheel travel trailer at Lou Ellen's parent's house. I took the truck to run some errands and left Lou Ellen with her folks so they could visit.

While I was out, the belt came loose from the engine. I pulled into a church parking lot. It appeared they were having choir rehearsal that night. A lot of people drove into the same parking lot and went into the church. I could hear them singing inside, singing about the Lord. Many of them saw me or at least my feet and backside as I was working on the engine. The hood was up. It was clear I was having trouble. But they had to hurry and get inside so they could sing and talk about serving the Lord.

I sang along with some of the songs as I struggled to replace the belt. I'm not a mechanic. I was finally finishing up as they came out and got into their cars. Not a single one of those good church folks asked if I was all right, needed help, or offered me a drink of water. I'm sure they had good excuses for not offering any help. They probably had important things to do, like getting home in time to watch their favorite TV programs or something. There is a difference, a big difference, between an excuse and a reason—a major difference.

How often do we praise the Lord, sing about the Lord, talk about the Lord but never get around to serving the Lord. Remember the words of Jesus: "Assuredly, I say unto you, in as much as you did not do it to one of the least of these, you did not do it unto Me" (Matthew 25:45).

I went into a bookstore in Greenville, South Carolina, back in the days when I was still a young pastor. I picked up a particular book I wanted to buy. I noticed the cover was damaged. It looked like someone had dropped it and damaged one of the corners. It was the only copy they had of that book, so I went ahead and took it to the counter to pay for it. When the cashier saw the damaged corner, she said she couldn't sell me a damaged book and would get me another one. When I told her there were no others on the shelf, she checked in the back. There were no other copies in the store. She took the book and put a sticker on it. The sticker said, "Damaged price reduced." She then marked the book down to half price.

When we substitute excuses for service, we become soiled, marred, damaged, and our service to the Lord is reduced.

The Good Samaritan helped the injured man not because he deserved to be helped or because he deserved to be loved but because he needed to be loved and cared for.

# 40

## Good Soil

### Matthew 13:1–9, 18–23

AT OUR FIRST pastorate in Kentucky, we had a dairy farmer we got really close to. I had picked out a garden spot close to the parsonage next to the creek. They had told me this creek never went dry, even in a drought.

They also told me I wouldn't be able to grow much there because the soil was a little hard and didn't have the proper nutrients. I told them I was going to try anyway.

I went to the dairy farmer and asked him if he would do me a favor. I asked if he would let me clean out his dairy barn, where the cows came in to be milked. We're talking about a lot of cows. He was more than pleased to let me do this. I told him I would have to borrow his truck. Then he realized what I was going to do.

I took all of that manure and scattered it all over my garden area. I then went to a chicken farmer and got a little chicken manure. I couldn't use much because it was too strong.

I also took all the leaves we raked up and scattered them across the garden area. I then had one of the farmers with a large tractor come and plow it up, mixing it all together. It sat there all winter, while the leaves rotted and mixed with the manure and dirt.

When spring came, the soil was rich, deep, moist, and ready to receive the seeds and plants.

I had it plowed up again and then began to plant. Oh, my goodness, it grew and produced more than we could handle. We canned a hundred quarts of green beans for ourselves and still gave some away. The potatoes grew big because the soil had become soft and fertile. We also had plenty of other vegetables.

That is what happens when the soil is good and prepared.

In the same way, our hearts must be prepared to receive God's word. Before opening the scriptures or taking part in a worship service, we should always pray for the Lord to open our hearts and make them a fertile ground to receive His word.

# 41

## Respect for the One True God

### Deuteronomy 5:1, 6–10

I ASKED A young lady in a tribal village of another country, "What do you worship?" I didn't ask her who, but what, as I knew most of them in the area were worshipping false gods of wood, stone, or even animals. She named one of the many gods they worshipped. I asked her, "Where is it?"

She told me it was in her hut.

I asked, "Where are you?"

She said, "Here."

I asked, "What if you need your god right now while you are here?"

She said she would go back to her hut. I asked her where did she get it. She told me her husband brought it home. I asked where he got it. She said he bought it in the market and brought it home. I then asked her what they would do if they wanted it outside for some reason. "How does it get out of their hut?"

She was getting a little impatient with me. She told me her husband would bring it outside. I asked how it would get back inside so they could pray at night. Now she was really getting tired of my questions, but wanting to get the supplies we were giving away, she answered that her husband would take it back inside, but they usually don't move it. It's easier to leave it in place. I said I had one final question, "If we bury it, how does it get out of the grave?"

The idea of doing such a thing bothered her, but she answered, "My husband would dig it out and clean it up."

I said, "It seems that your god depends on your husband and can't do anything for itself." She told me she had never thought of it like that. I said, "Let me tell you about the One that is with you wherever you go. He died for you and came out of the grave for you." As we continued to talk, she became a faithful follower of Jesus.

I heard someone say, "If you have a created image, you possess it. But God possesses us. He bought us with a price." How true that is.

# 42

## Traps

### Luke 15:17

THE VENUS FLYTRAP is one of God's unique creations. It's native to South Carolina, North Carolina, and Florida. It has a sweet nectar that draws the insects. Inside it has six trigger hairs. When these hairs are touched, the plant closes. The unsuspecting fly smells the nectar and decides to have a snack. When he crawls into the opened plant, he touches the trigger hairs, which causes the plant to close. The plant then eats the fly.

I can imagine the young fly as it flies over the Venus flytrap.

"What was that? It smelled so good."

So he comes back for another look. He sees it. It smells so good. That nectar would taste so good. So he lands on the edge of the plant. But then he remembers. Mother fly said, "Stay away from plants like this."

Daddy fly said, "Stay away from plants like this."

At fly school, they showed pictures and said, "Stay away from plants like this."

The fly handbook said, "Stay away from plants like this."

*But it smells and looks so good. I'm here by myself. No one will ever know. I'll just take a little bite.*

## WHERE ARE WE GOING TODAY, LORD?

So he crawls into the plant to enjoy the nectar. As he does, he triggers one of the little hairs in the plant, and in an instant, the plant closes, and it is too late. The plant eats the fly.

When the prodigal son in Luke 15 was at home, he thought, *If I just had money, I could make it in the far country.* He could smell the sweet nectar and wanted it.

One evening, Lou Ellen and I were sitting in our RV. She was sitting on the sofa across from me. As we were talking, I saw a mouse run just behind her feet, along the edge of the sofa. I mainly saw its tale, but I saw enough to know what it was. I immediately silently prayed, "Lord, please don't let her see that mouse." If she'd seen it, we probably would have had a new sunroof as she would jump up. I knew I was going to have to get rid of it.

The next morning, as I was going out to meet with the pastor of the church we were in revival with, she said, "Honey, please pick up a mouse trap while you are out. I saw some droppings this morning. I think we have a mouse in the house, and I'm not sharing the house with a mouse."

I said, "A mouse. Why would a mouse be traveling in an RV?"

She told me to just make sure I got the trap.

When I came back in a few hours later, she asked, "Did you get the trap?"

"Yep, I got it."

That night, after the services, as we were about to go to bed, she reminded me to put the trap out. I got some peanut butter and put it on the trap. I use peanut butter because it won't easily come off, and they seem to like it. I prefer crunchy. As I went over to place the trap next to the sofa, she wanted to know what was I doing putting it next to the sofa. She explained putting it next to the cabinets would be better. It would be closer to the food. That is where he would be. After a discussion on the best place to put the trap, I simply told her I was placing it next to the sofa. I just had a feeling it might be passing that way.

After setting the trap, we went to bed. Now I was not in there when the mouse came out and really don't know what he was thinking. But I imagine, when we went to bed and turned the lights off, he said something like, "Finally. I thought they never would go to bed. I was getting hungry." Then he comes out. "That smells like peanut butter. I love peanut butter." As he gets closer, he realizes it is peanut butter. Not only that, it's crunchy, which is his favorite too. When he sees it, he remembers mother mouse said to stay away from things like this. Daddy mouse said to stay away from things like this. At mouse school, they said to stay away from things like this. The mouse handbook said to stay away from things like this. But it looks so good. No one will ever know. So he steps forward and takes a bite. For a moment, a very brief moment, it tastes good. But then, *bam*! In an instant, it is all over. We must remember what someone said many years ago, "Sin will take you further than you want to go, keep you longer than you want to stay, and cost you more than you want to pay."

As we were lying in bed, we both heard the sound of the trap going off. We knew we caught him. I couldn't help myself. I turned toward my wife and said, "I told you so." I then confessed that I had seen the mouse the previous night and knew his path.

We must always remember that God's word is not to restrict us but to give us freedom. God knows best and knows how we were designed to live, and His word is to protect us. If we would only listen.

# 43

## Will the Real Underdog Please Stand Up?

### First Samuel 1–51

A LONG TIME ago, when I was about twenty-one, maybe twenty-two, I was serving as minister of music and youth. I had taken our youth to a summer camp. One of the activities was a tennis tournament for those who wanted to enter. It was mixed doubles. That means there would be two on each team: one a male and the other a female. The staff and counselors would be able to compete and play with the youth. You could pick your own partners. The teams were divided into two groups. One group would challenge teams from the other group. We were in the group that was to challenge a team from the other group.

It so happened that in our youth group was a young lady who played on our local high school tennis team. She was very good. I teamed up with her. Now we only had to find a team to challenge. As I was sitting in the stands. watching someone else play, I noticed a man sitting on the row behind me. He seemed to be enjoying the match. I also noticed he was an older guy. He looked to be in his late forties, maybe fifties. I asked him if he played tennis. He said not as much as he would like to. He told me he was happy he would get to play here. He told me he had entered the tournament. I asked who his partner was. When he told me her name, I smiled inside. I had met her before. She was his age, maybe a little older, and not athletic-looking at all. I was thinking this could be an easy first match. I was in my prime physically and had an excellent young partner. While I hadn't been playing tennis long, I felt we could certainly handle these older folks. I issued the challenge.

Later that afternoon, we walked onto the court. I was feeling confident. The man was going to serve for them. My partner went up to the net as I stood at the back of the court, waiting for his serve. He was bumbling around with the balls like he hadn't done it many times before. It was a little comical. I thought I would take it easy on them. As he started to serve, I only halfway prepared myself because I really didn't think it would be that difficult. But as he threw the ball up to hit it with his racket, I couldn't help but notice the change in his movements. His form looked so good. The tennis ball shot by me like a bullet. What just happened? He was ready to serve again. This time I got ready. I wasn't going to get caught off guard again. It didn't matter. He was far more than I could handle. For the most part, his partner just stood back, letting him handle us. She didn't have to do much. He was all over the court. The crowd was having a great time watching us get destroyed. I couldn't help but laugh as well. I knew I had been duped.

As we were walking off the court, a man walked up to me and said, "I guess you were this year's victim." He had been listening to our conversation in the stands when I made the challenge. He told me the fellow spent his lunch hour practicing his serve. He wasn't lying when he said he didn't play as much as he would like because he would like to play every day. He also told me he played in semipro tournaments and that he loved playing against and beating young folks.

I thought, going into the match, that our opponents were the underdogs. Most people thought so as well. But it soon became evident who the real underdogs were. We didn't know it, but we were in trouble as soon as we walked onto the court.

In First Samuel 17, we often talk of David as the underdog. We love to pull for the underdog. But David was not the underdog. Goliath was, even though no one seemed to know it. Goliath was already in trouble. He just didn't know it. David wasn't the underdog. He was the mighty dog.

When we go out under the leadership of the Holy Spirit, we may appear to be the underdog when in reality we are not.

# 44

## It's Not the Wires

### First Corinthians 3:6

I AM GRATEFUL for the wires in the church that bring power for the lights, AC, heat, etc. I remember one of the first outdoor services we had because of COVID-19. It was cold, and my fingers were hurting. I've messed them up through the years, so they do not do well when it gets cold. Then right before we came back inside (after nineteen weeks of outside services), I was beginning to sweat during the services because of the heat. Spring had arrived.

But the wires are not the source of the power that brings us the heat and AC. The power flows through them.

I remember well lying on a very hard bed, looking up at the ceiling fan overhead. There was no air-conditioning. It was extremely hot and humid. Though I was next to a window, there was no breeze.

As I looked up at the fan, I noticed it beginning to slow down. I was pleading with it not to stop, but it got slower and slower until it stopped, and there was no breeze coming from it. I was in a tribal area where the power would often run out before it got to us. The wires were still there, but there was not any power coming through them to make the fan work. The wires were not the power. They were the conduit, which the power ran through.

Paul, in writing this letter to the Corinthians, wanted them to understand that it was not him or Apollos but God that gave the increase. The church should be focused on God for what He was doing and not on any person whom God may be using.

Paul and Apollos would have been fruitless no matter how hard they worked had God not given the increase.

Lord, never let me forget that any ministry I have been called to carry out does not belong to me, nor does any success I may have had come from my power but from the Holy Spirit, which flows through me. Big stage, little stage—I'm just thrilled and excited to have a place to serve the One Who has done so much for me.

In one city we served in, there was a church that was referred to as Bill's (not real name) church. If you asked anyone who went to that church, "What church do you go to?" they would say, "I go to Bill's church." On the church sign outside of the church, his name was written as big or even bigger than the church's name.

The church doesn't belong to us. It doesn't belong to the pastor, staff, deacons, the one who gives the most, or any individual or group. It's His church. He is the One who founded it. He is the One Who died for it. He is to be our focus.

# 45

## Psalm 51

SHORTLY AFTER GOING into missions and evangelism, Lou Ellen and I were asked to go with a church youth group on a ski retreat. It was the week between Christmas and New Year's. We were to lead the Bible studies each day. It worked out good for us because the weeks between Thanksgiving and New Year's were usually open as churches generally didn't have revivals or conferences during the holiday season.

    I learned to water-ski when I was little but had never skied on snow. After a while, I was getting the hang of it and decided I would try one of the more advanced slopes. It turned out to be more advanced than I thought. It was beautiful riding the ski lift up the slope. While I was enjoying the beauty of all the snow on the trees, I began to realize this is not going to be as easy as I thought. I was about two-thirds of the way down the slope and hadn't fallen. I was having a great time and beginning to feel pretty confident. I was enjoying the scenery, as well as the skiing. That's when it happened. I came to a sharp turn. I mean really sharp. I crashed. Nothing was broken, so I got up and continued down the mountain. When I got to the bottom, I got back on the ski lift and went back up. I was determined to make it all the way down without falling. I was really doing well this time. I was navigating all the regular turns without any trouble. But then I came to the turn that took me out before. I was going to make it this time. Maybe not. As I was halfway through the blind turn, I saw her. A young girl had fallen. She was right in the middle of the slope. She looked to be late teens or early twenties. She was lying on the ground, stretched out across the trail, trying to get up. I was headed right for her. Down I went. I didn't want to hurt her, so I threw myself to the ground. I lost one of my skis but managed to fall without hitting her or getting hurt. She started to apologize for causing me to fall, but I assured her it wasn't the first time. That's when we heard a group of guys coming down the slope. Five or six college buddies were racing down the slope and were about to come around the turn. We both tried to get out of the way, but they came around so fast. They had nowhere to go. One boy was slightly ahead of the others and took me out as I had just managed to get to my feet. Now there were three of us spread out across the trail. Two more came around the bend, and down they went. As they came around the turn, the big smiles on their faces turned to fear as they saw us piled up across the trail. It was over quick. One minute we were enjoying the trip down the slope, and then in a matter of seconds, we were all piled up in the snow. Fortunately, no one was seriously hurt, just a few bruises. We put our skies back on and finished the trip down the slope.

When I got to the bottom, I thought about going back up. I had almost made it—maybe if I tried one more time. Maybe not. It was getting late, and the snow was beginning to ice over. The Lord had given me a good day of skiing with no injuries. My knees were tired and sore. I was not going to injure them and not be able to run anymore. That was my one and only day of skiing, but it had been fun.

The massive pileup of skiers all started when the first lady fell. That started it all. That is what sin does. Once started, it continues to grow.

# About the Author

Jim and Lou Ellen both surrendered to the ministry in their teens. They met during their first year at Anderson College (now Anderson University–Anderson, South Carolina). They began serving together when Jim accepted the call to his first church as minister of music. It was during this time Jim joined the United States Marines so he could both serve his country and, after a time of active duty, continue his education for the ministry.

After eight years in the music and youth ministry, Jim returned to school to get his seminary degree. He served after seventeen years as a senior pastor. From the beginning, Jim knew the Lord was preparing him for missions and evangelism. In 1998, under the leadership of the Holy Spirit, Jim and Lou Ellen formed Winning Our World (WOW) Ministries.

They lived twenty-two years full-time in an RV as they traveled across America, leading revivals, conferences, and helping churches. They have been from Key West, Florida, to Seattle, Washington. Jim made several trips to Zimbabwe, where he taught seminary classes in Harare and Victoria Falls. They returned to Victoria Falls together, where Lou Ellen led a ladies' conference and Jim co-led a pastors' conference. Jim has made multiple trips to India to help establish a children's and widows' home. He has also conducted Christian leadership conferences across India. He has taken part in crusades in South Africa. Jim has been in forty-two states and fifteen counties. Jim has also served as a coach/consultant for the South Carolina Baptist Convention. He served two terms as president of the South Carolina Evangelists Network.

Today, with over fifty years of ministry experience, Jim serves as a transitional pastor, as well as holding an occasional revival while continuing their work in India and mentoring young ministers. He loves spending time with his wife (who has been by his side throughout their ministry), his children, and grandchildren.